MASTERING VOCABULARY

BOOK TWO

Vicki Tyler

CAMBRIDGE Adult Education
Prentice Hall Regents, Englewood Cliffs, NJ 07632

Cambridge gratefully acknowledges the advice and contributions of the following adult educators who reviewed the draft version of this book:

Susan Adamowski, Assistant Dean, School of Continuing Education, Triton Community College, River Grove, Illinois
Marion E. Myers, Assistant Director of Programs for the Military—Atlantic Division, City Colleges of Chicago, Norfolk, Virginia
Stephen J. Steurer, Correctional Programs Specialist, National Institute for Corrections, Washington, D.C.

EXECUTIVE EDITOR:	Brian Schenk
DEVELOPMENTAL EDITOR:	Marjorie P. K. Weiser
PRODUCTION MANAGER:	Arthur Michalez
MANAGING EDITOR:	Eileen Guerrin

Cover Design by Richard Shen

Printed in the United States of America

10 9 8 7 6 5 4 3 2

ISBN 0-8428-0181-2

Prentice-Hall International (UK) Limited, *London*
Prentice-Hall of Australia Pty. Limited, *Sydney*
Prentice-Hall Canada Inc., *Toronto*
Prentice-Hall Hispanoamericana, S.A., *Mexico*
Prentice-Hall of India Private Limited, *New Delhi*
Prentice-Hall of Japan, Inc., *Tokyo*
Simon & Schuster Asia Pte. Ltd., *Singapore*
Editora Prentice-Hall do Brasil, Ltda., *Rio de Janeiro*

TABLE OF CONTENTS

TO THE READER

This book is about your language. There is no limit to the ways in which language can be put together for original effect and fresh meaning. At any moment, you may be thinking a sentence that no human being ever created before!

Words are powerful. Wisely chosen, words can put your message across. They can get you a promotion at work, elect you to office, win you friends and lovers. Rashly chosen, words can cost you your job, lose the election, turn off friends and lovers.

The words you use are your vocabulary. They are a tool for communicating. A tool is only as good as the skill of its user. In the "golden hands" of a skilled user, a penknife, a paintbrush, or a needle and thread can produce masterpieces. Words, too, when strung together by a skilled user, give us the masterpieces of our literature. Spoken, they give us treasures of oratory and theater. Vocabulary is a tool that everyone can learn to use well.

This book will help you become a skilled user of vocabulary. It will show you how to get the same message across in different situations, how to say the same thing in different ways, how to avoid saying something that's not quite what you want to say—and more. You can read MASTERING VOCABULARY, BOOK TWO, from start to finish, practicing and doing exercises as you come to them. Or you can find a topic of relevance or choice to focus on. Jump about in the book until you find what you need today, what might be of interest tomorrow.

Chapter 1 will help you understand the unique aspects of communication among human beings, and tell you how a knowledge of vocabulary can make your communications more precise. It will also give you an overview of the rest of the book. Chapter 2 will show you that English comes in many varieties, and that different words are appropriate to different situations. Chapter 3 will give you fresh words for sharper meanings, and show you how to avoid stale, overworked words. In Chapter 4 you will learn how *not* to choose wrong words, those that sound like the ones you really want to use. Chapter 4 will also help you spell the word you do want correctly. When words are put on paper, spelling counts. Chapter 5 will improve your spelling to represent your true vocabulary. Each of these chapters contains practice exercises throughout, and ends with a set of Exercises for Review. These can be used to reinforce the instruction in the chapter, or to measure your expanded vocabulary skills. Check your answers against the separate Answer Key.

Chapter 6 contains Mastery Tests for topics covered in Chapters 2 through 5. These can be used in varied ways. For example, to find out which chapter will help you the most, try using some of the exercises in Chapter 6 as diagnostic tests. (You might, for example, try tests A and C under each main heading.) Check your answers against the separate Answer Key; if you had major problems, study the appropriate chapter(s). You can also use the Mastery Tests at intervals after completing a chapter and the exercises contained in it; this will show you how well you have retained what you learned. To test vocabulary retention in this way, do the appropriate exercises in Chapter 6 two weeks or one month after you complete each chapter.

This book is really about COMMUNICATION. When you have finished it, your skills as a communicator will be sharpened. Your writing and your speaking will be improved. You will be a skilled user of the most versatile tool any human being can have—words.

TO THE INSTRUCTOR

This is a vocabulary-enrichment book. It is designed to be used either in a classroom setting or for individual study. Exercises for Review in the four instructional chapters, instruction-reinforcing tests throughout those chapters, and an entire chapter of Mastery Tests, give you great flexibility in designing programs to meet your students' needs. You may select from the review exercises in the chapters to use as diagnostics, assigning chapters for instruction and reinforcement exercises as needed. Then you can use the Mastery Tests as unit review exercises. Or you may select from the Mastery Tests for your diagnostics. The information and exercises can be adapted to virtually any instructional setting. The separate Answer Key is arranged in the same sequence as the exercises in this book, making the answers easy to locate for learner and instructor alike. Cambridge, The Adult Education Company hopes you and your students will enjoy using this book. You might also want to look at MASTERING VOCABULARY, BOOK ONE, which teaches basic approaches to vocabulary building.

1. LANGUAGE: THE HUMAN HERITAGE

Our language is our heritage as human beings. Our ability to communicate is what makes us truly and distinctively human. Other animals send and receive messages. But their communications do not begin to approach the complex exchange of ideas made possible by human speech and writing. Language is a rich and varied tool that we can use to create precise, imaginative, informative, and highly personal messages. Language connects us with the people around us. It also allows us to pass information along from one generation to the next. When we read, we can share the knowledge and ideas of those who came before us. And in our writing we can add to and build on those ideas.

We can experience the wisdom and beauty to be found in the Bible or the works of Shakespeare:

> To every thing there is a season, and a time to every purpose under heaven.
>
> *Ecclesiastes*

> To be, or not to be: that is the question:
> Whether 'tis nobler in the mind to suffer
> The slings and arrows of outrageous fortune,
> Or to take arms against a sea of troubles,
> And by opposing end them?
>
> William Shakespeare,
> *Hamlet*

We can be present at the birth of important scientific or social ideas:

> To every action there is always opposed an equal reaction: or, the mutual actions of two bodies upon each other are always equal, and directed to contrary parts.
>
> Sir Isaac Newton,
> *Laws of Motion*, 1687

> It would be an endless task to trace the variety of meannesses, cares, and sorrows into which women are plunged by the prevailing opinion that they are created rather to feel than reason, and that all the power they obtain must be obtained by their charms and weakness.
>
> Mary Wollstonecraft,
> *A Vindication of the Rights of Woman,* 1792

We can appreciate the personality of a fictional character from another time and place:

> It appeared, indeed, from the countenance of this proprietor, that he was of a frank, but hasty and choleric, temper.
>
> Sir Walter Scott,
> *Ivanhoe,* 1819

We can share a joke with Mark Twain:

> Nothing so needs reforming as other people's habits.
>
> *Pudd'nhead Wilson,* 1894

Or we can share a moment of reflection with Emily Dickinson:

> Hope is the thing with feathers—
> That perches in the soul—
> And sings the tune without the words—
> And never stops—at all.
>
> #254, c. 1861

Our language is our heritage. It is a connection to our past and our future. When we enrich our vocabularies, we deepen our understanding of our language. We strengthen our connection to the generations of readers and writers who have come before us. We increase our capacity to share other people's experiences and learn from them. And we improve our ability to share our ideas and experiences with others.

Language Is Power

Language is more than a link to the past, of course. It helps us to be effective participants in today's world.

Language gives us a sense of belonging. Being part of any group means learning to "speak its language." To be accepted in certain social groups, for example, you must know the slang that "insiders" speak. To function in certain jobs, you must learn the special vocabularies, or jargon, of those jobs. To succeed in many areas of American society, you must know the rules and vocabulary of standard English—the language of "educated" people.

To be effective, the language we use must be appropriate to the occasion and to the audience we want to reach. Some types of language can reach a broader audience than others. In Chapter 2 of this book, you will study several varieties of English and how each is used. You will learn when it is appropriate to use slang, jargon, and euphemisms, and when it is not. You will learn to identify standard, informal, and substandard usages. You will practice maintaining a consistent tone and level of language in your writing. You will also become aware of ways we can change the language to make it fairer and more inclusive of various groups in society.

Making Word Power Work for You

Words persuade, entertain, inform, tell a story. They give you the power to influence the world around you. To be successful, however, your language must be not only appropriate, but also vivid and precise. The right words can win an election, settle an argument, make a friend, change a mind, make someone laugh, or clinch a business deal. The wrong words can confuse, offend, or simply bore your audience.

In any given situation, you can choose among a wide variety of words to convey the same or a similar message. Some choices are vague and colorless. Others are vivid and precise. Choosing a colorful word and being sure of its exact meaning take practice. Chapter 3 will give you a chance to practice matching the right word to the right situation. You will learn about the denotations and connotations of words. And you will learn how to use the thesaurus and the dictionary to expand your vocabulary of words that are similar in meaning but whose shades of difference are important. Choosing words carefully is a habit you can begin by doing the exercises in this book.

Getting It Right

In Chapters 4 and 5 you will practice some basic skills important to getting your message across in standard English. If you have already used MASTERING VOCABULARY, Book One, these chapters may at first glance seem familiar. But you will find that they go a step further than similar ones in the previous book. In Chapter 4 of this book, you will learn to use more than 150 homonyms and other confusing words correctly. Long after you've finished the exercises in this chapter, you'll still refer to it again and again as a handy glossary of words that can confuse even careful writers from time to time.

In Chapter 5 you will strengthen your spelling skills by practicing a "trouble-shooting" technique—a strategy for zeroing in on problem spots in frequently misspelled words. You will also learn the meaning and spelling of words frequently used in six special fields—law, business and finance, politics and government, health and medicine, food and cooking, and the arts.

Chapter 6 is a collection of Mastery Tests that will reinforce every important concept you studied in Chapters 2 through 5. They'll also test your memory of new words you will have learned along the way. In Chapter 6 and, indeed, throughout this book, you'll find puzzles and games that allow you to "play" with words as you learn them. Although these exercises are fun to do, they are also serious study aids. Playing with words is one of the best—and most enjoyable—ways to familiarize yourself with them. So enjoy yourself with a clear conscience as you enrich your vocabulary and spelling skills!

2. THE VARIETIES OF ENGLISH: CHOOSING APPROPRIATE LANGUAGE

Nobody uses the same kind of language all the time. Most of us use one kind of language when we're talking with our friends and a different kind when we're talking to our employers or writing a business letter. If we were ever to give a speech at the United Nations, we wouldn't use the same kinds of words we use to tell a funny story at a party. The way we express ourselves in a letter to a friend is even slightly different from the way we'd talk to that person on the telephone.

USE WORDS THAT ARE APPROPRIATE TO THE SITUATION

Language experts have compared levels of language to a person's wardrobe. Most of us have different kinds of clothes for different occasions. We wouldn't wear a bathing suit to a wedding. We may set aside certain clothes for exercising or working on the car. If we work in an office, we may dress more formally on the job than we do at home. In short, many of our clothes are appropriate for some situations, but not others. So it is with language. Some situations call for very formal speech or writing, while others are very informal. Still others call for something in between these extremes.

Other Kinds of Appropriateness

Deciding when to use the language that fits various social levels is only one part of our choice of appropriate words. Another issue concerns the use of **jargon,** the specialized vocabulary used by people with a shared expertise or common interest (computers, sports, photography, or gourmet cooking, for example). When is jargon appropriate and when is it inappropriate? Are **regionalisms**—words and expressions limited to a certain geographic area—to be cherished or avoided? Still another issue is whether it is ever appropriate to use **euphemisms**—inoffensive words for unpleasant realities. And what about the changing standards of appropriateness and social reality reflected in replacing *stewardess* with *flight attendant, mailman* with *letter carrier,* and *fireman* with *firefighter*? Think about these questions as you read. We will explore all these issues in this chapter as we look at the many varieties of our English language.

LEVELS OF LANGUAGE

Instinctively you probably realize that there are some words and phrases that are best not used in certain situations. After reading this description of the four major levels of language—**formal, standard, informal,** and **substandard**—you will have a better knowledge of what language is suited to what occasions, as well as what language should be avoided on *any* occasion.

Formal

Formal language uses abstract nouns and other words not commonly heard in everyday conversation or encountered in our casual reading. Such words are selected not only to achieve the precision of meaning demanded by the author's purpose and subject matter, but also to create a certain tone.

Formal language is characterized by its sentence structures as well as its vocabulary. It often consists of sentences that are fairly long and that may contain many carefully related ideas. Here are some examples of written and spoken formal language:

> Because seizures are executed principally to secure evidence, and because such evidence generally has utility in our legal system only in the context of a trial supervised by a judge, it is apparent that the admission of legally obtained evidence implicates the same constitutional concerns as the initial seizure of that evidence.
>
> Justice William J. Brennan, Jr.,
> Opinion in the case of
> *U.S. v. Leon*

> A novel is balanced between a few true impressions and the multitude of false ones that make up most of what we call life. It tells us that for every human being there is a diversity of existences, that the single existence is itself an illusion in part, that these many existences signify

> something, tend to something, fulfill something; it promises us meaning, harmony, and even justice.
>
> Saul Bellow,
> Speech upon receiving the Nobel Prize

> When in the course of human events, it becomes necessary for one people to dissolve the political bonds which have connected them with another, and to assume among the powers of the earth the separate and equal station which the laws of nature and of nature's God entitle them, a decent respect to the opinion of mankind requires that they should declare the causes which impel them to the separation. . . .
>
> Thomas Jefferson,
> *Declaration of Independence*

These days formal language is more often written than spoken, and it is usually intended for a limited audience. Scholars and people in certain professions use formal language in the books and articles they write for their colleagues. Laws are written in formal English, and other government documents use this level of language too.

Not all formal English is "good" English. Much academic and legal writing, for example, is rightly criticized for being unnecessarily wordy and often unclear. Some writers overdo formal language to the extent that the simplest ideas become entangled in a mass of incomprehensible long words and unessential phrases. Such writing is often called "gobbledygook." In 1984, for example, a Federal judge ordered the government to remove such language from Medicare forms and correspondence on the grounds that it was misleading "officialese" that did not "qualify as English." The ruling was based on a case in which a man had written to find out the cause of discrepancies in his wife's Medicare benefits. Here is an excerpt from the letter the man received in reply:

> Approved charges are determined by each Medicare carrier. The amounts are based on statistics covering customary charges of an individual physician and prevailing rates by all physicians rendering similar services in a given locality. However, increases in prevailing charges for doctor's services are limited from year to year by an "economic index" formula. This formula does not limit the amount a doctor may charge a patient. It only limits the amount Medicare can pay.

The judge decided that the man had reason to be more confused than ever after receiving this supposedly clarifying letter.

In an effort to show off their vocabularies, some people use excessively formal language that is inappropriate to most situations. They forget that using simple, unpretentious language is often the most effective way to get a message across. Unless you are a graduate student or in a profession that requires formal writing, not much of your communication will be done on the formal level. Mastering standard English is much more important and useful.

Standard

Standard English, the language that educated people use for most of their writing, steers a middle course between formal and informal language. While based on the rules of grammar and usage taught in schools, its vocabulary is simpler than that of formal English although not as relaxed as casual conversation. Formal and standard English are both less changeable than informal; therefore, they are considered "safer" for any writing that is meant to be of lasting value.

Most books, magazines, and newspapers for a general audience are written in standard English. This is also the form of the language you would use in a business letter, at a job interview, or in a conversation with someone you did not know well and wanted to impress favorably. Standard English is considered the "prestige dialect" of the United States, and mastering it is a necessary prerequisite to succeeding in many occupations.

This book is written in standard English. Here are some other examples:

> In her towering presence, the Statue of Liberty displays the artistic and engineering genius of the 19th century at its best.
>
> *Discovery*, July 1984, p. 25

> Many people still hope for the emergence of an old-style, dynamic "great leader," but television is making it virtually impossible to find one.
>
> *Psychology Today*, July 1984, p. 47

> Manufacturers, under pressure to provide detailed health labels on their products, have often found that it is easier to work with consumer groups than against them.
>
> *The New York Times*, May 20, 1984

Informal

Informal language is usually spoken, rather than written. It is the level of language that most people use for their casual conversations, and it includes many usages the dictionary labels *colloquial* or *slang*. Here is an example of informal speech:

"I really gave him a piece of my mind. I told him to stop snooping into my affairs and he promised to quit."

"Do you think he's on the level?"

"No way."

Many professional writers do slip some informal usages into their writing when they want to sound conversational and folksy. The following headline from *People* magazine about young Prince William of England is an example of the folksy approach:

DI'S TYKE HITS THE "TERRIBLE TWOS"

Most of us use some informal language in our own writing, too, although informal writing can never be quite the same as informal speech. When you're talking to someone, you can use tone of voice and facial expressions to help get your message across. And if the other person is confused about your message, he or she can ask for more information and give you another chance to explain what you mean. In writing, on the other hand, you have to "spell things out" as clearly as possible, because your words alone have to do the job and you only have one chance to get your message across.

When your writing is addressed to a person or persons you don't know, you have to be especially careful. You can't make too many assumptions about which informal expressions your audience will understand and approve. That's one reason writers are discouraged from using too much slang in their work.

Slang expressions are informal usages that start out as the "in" language of a certain group. Many of our slang expressions (*rip off, to be together, mellow*) come from Black English. Teenagers too have their special vocabularies. Their language is a rich source of slang. In the 1960s they gave the language *far out, freak out,* and *groovy*. Today's teenagers have their own equivalents.

These "secret" languages help give a group a sense of identity. These terms brand insiders and outsiders. Gradually, though, many of the expressions slip into general use, and the insiders may replace them with new ones.

Slang can enrich the language. A good slang term such as *hotshot* or *fussbudget* expresses in one word an idea that previously may have taken many words to explain. Slang often communicates old ideas in a colorful or amusing way. The expressions *laid-back* and *uptight*, for example, may be overused, but they do create pictures in our minds of two very different types of people. And the expressions *blowing a gasket* or *flying off the handle* describe the explosive emotion of anger in a vivid, though unusual, way. Obviously, you wouldn't use these expressions to write a serious report, essay, or letter to the editor. They would be inappropriate in tone. Some slang may even be considered vulgar or offensive by some readers.

Slang is often just a fad. Many slang words don't stay popular for very long. Few things can bother a reader as much as outdated slang, and the last thing a writer wants to do is "turn off" a reader. That's why levels of language are so important.

Before moving on to the fourth level of English, substandard, try to identify the formal, standard, and informal language in the following exercise.

EXERCISE 1: Label each passage as *formal, informal,* or *standard.*

__________ **1.** "Billy Dee Williams won't come cheap to *Dynasty* next fall when he debuts as Diahann Carroll's hubby . . ." —*People,* June 25, 1984, p. 29

__________ **2.** "The greater the importance of safeguarding the community from incitements to the overthrow of our institutions by force and violence, the more imperative is the need to preserve inviolate the constitutional rights of free speech, free press, and free assembly. . . ."—Justice Charles Evans Hughes, Opinion in the case of *DeJonge v. Oregon,* 1937

__________ **3.** "The potato is a remarkable food. It contains so well-balanced an array of nutrients that people can live on virtually nothing else for years on end."—*Natural History,* March 1984, p. 12

__________ **4.** How do jocks stay psyched up when the breaks of the game go against them?

__________ **5.** "Among Balanchine's masterpieces, there are those which are especially prized—not only admired but loved."—*New Yorker,* June 4, 1984, p. 106

__________ **6.** "The imperatives of technology and organization, not the images of ideology, are what determine the shape of economic society."—John Kenneth Galbraith, *The New Industrial State,* 1978

Substandard

Substandard English is any usage that violates the rules of standard English. This level of English is spoken by people who either are uneducated or do not feel at home with the rules of standard English they learned in school. Substandard English is not necessarily "bad," but if you want to get ahead in business, the professions, or the academic world, you must learn to avoid it, especially in your writing.

Substandard is characterized chiefly by incorrect forms of verbs (*you was, he don't, I seen*), pronouns (*hisself,* confusion of *whose* and *who's,* etc.), and adverbs (*I worked real hard*) as well as double negatives (*I don't have none*) and other usages that are considered "improper" by usage experts. A good grammar and usage handbook is your best guide to avoiding such mistakes. In addition, look out for the following words and expressions that will brand your writing as substandard:

ain't: Do not use as a substitute for *isn't, aren't,* or *am not*. There is no contraction for *am not*. The correct forms are *it* (*he* or *she*) *isn't, we aren't, I'm not.*

anywheres, anyways, nowheres: The correct forms are *anywhere, anyway,* and *nowhere.*

anywhere
EXAMPLES: She couldn't find it ~~anywheres~~.

anyway
I didn't need it ~~anyways~~.

being as, being as how: Use *since* or *because* instead.

Since
EXAMPLE: ~~Being as how~~ you really seem sorry, I'll forgive you.

but what: Use *that* instead.

that
EXAMPLE: There was no doubt ~~but what~~ she could win.

hadn't ought: Use *ought not* instead.

ought not
EXAMPLE: You ~~hadn't ought~~ to drive through red lights.

irregardless: The correct word is *regardless.*

Regardless
EXAMPLE: ~~Irregardless~~ of your criticisms, I still believe it's an excellent film.

see where, read where, hear where: Do not use these expressions to mean "notice" or "find out." Use *that* instead of *where.*

that
EXAMPLE: I see ~~where~~ the networks are planning their fall schedules.

EXERCISE 2: The following paragraph contains six examples of substandard usage. Cross out each incorrect word or expression. Then rewrite the paragraph, replacing each substandard usage with standard English.

I ain't sure what happened on my favorite TV show last night being as how I wasn't home to watch it. I don't doubt but what it was an exciting program. Irregardless, it couldn't of been as exciting as the basketball game I seen.

USAGE LABELS

A good dictionary labels words and expressions that are considered colloquial or slang. For example, in *Webster's New World Dictionary,* the word *stuffy,* meaning "dull," is labeled colloquial, while the expression *stuffed shirt* is considered slang.

You can use these labels as a guide to choosing appropriate words for your writing. Words labeled colloquial are appropriate for informal writing, but are probably not the best choices for writing that has a serious purpose or serious subject matter. Words labeled slang are more questionable still. Before you use any slang words in your writing, consider carefully whether they might disrupt the tone and impression you are trying to create. If the dictionary does not label a word or expression, you can assume that usage is good standard English.

Read the excerpt on page 13 from *Webster's New World Dictionary, Second College Edition.* Note how some usages of the word *knock* and expressions formed from it are labeled [Colloq.] or [Slang]. Then try Exercise 3.

EXERCISE 3: Read each sentence below and notice how the italicized word or expression is used. Label each usage as *slang, colloquial,* or *standard.* Refer to the dictionary excerpt for *knock* if necessary.

______________ **1.** If you haven't read the book, don't *knock* it.

______________ **2.** I told those kids to *knock it off!*

______________ **3.** Someone is *knocking* at the door.

______________ **4.** Let's *knock off* at four o'clock and go home.

______________ **5.** The owner *knocked* ten dollars off the price.

______________ **6.** The engine is developing a *knock.*

knock (näk) *vi.* [ME. *knokken* < OE. *cnocian*, akin to ON. *knoka*, MHG. *knochen*, to press < echoic base whence KNACK] **1.** to strike a blow or blows with the fist or some hard object; esp., to rap on a door **2.** to bump; collide; clash **3.** to make a thumping, pounding, or rattling noise: said of an engine, etc. ☆**4.** [Colloq.] to find fault; criticize adversely ☆**5.** *Gin Rummy* to end a deal by exposing one's hand and showing a surplus of not more than ten points in unmatched cards —*vt.* **1.** to hit; strike **2.** to make by hitting or striking [to *knock* a hole in a wall] ☆**3.** [Colloq.] to find fault with; criticize adversely —*n.* **1.** the act of knocking **2.** a hit; sharp or resounding blow; rap, as on a door **3.** a thumping or rattling noise in an engine, etc., as because of faulty combustion ☆**4.** [Colloq.] an adverse criticism **5.** [Colloq.] a misfortune or trouble [the school of hard *knocks*] —*SYN.* see STRIKE —**knock about** (or **around**) [Colloq.] **1.** to wander about; roam **2.** to treat roughly —**knock back** [Colloq.] to gulp down (an alcoholic drink) —**knock down** **1.** to hit so as to cause to fall ☆**2.** to take apart for convenience in shipping **3.** to indicate the sale of (an article) at an auction, as by a blow of the auctioneer's hammer **4.** [Slang] to earn as pay —☆**knock for a loop** [Slang] **1.** to punch very hard **2.** to make a deep impression on —☆**knock it off!** [Slang] stop doing that! specif., stop talking! —**knock off** **1.** to hit so as to cause to fall **2.** [Colloq.] *a*) to stop working *b*) to leave off (work) **3.** [Colloq.] to deduct **4.** [Colloq.] to do; accomplish ☆**5.** [Slang] to kill, overcome, etc. —☆**knock (oneself) out** to make great efforts; exhaust oneself —**knock out** **1.** *Boxing* to defeat (an opponent) by knocking him to the ground so that he cannot rise within a specified time **2.** *a*) to make unconscious *b*) to make exhausted; tire out **3.** to defeat, destroy, etc. **4.** [Colloq.] to do; make; specif., to compose, write, etc., esp. casually or with careless haste —☆**knock out of the box** *Baseball* to make so many hits against (an opposing pitcher) as to cause his removal —**knock over** [Slang] ☆to rob —**knock together** **1.** to cause to collide **2.** to make or compose hastily or crudely

______________ **7.** The bad news *knocked me for a loop.*

______________ **8.** Do your best but don't *knock yourself out.*

______________ **9.** I think I can *knock out* my term paper over the weekend.

______________ **10.** Duran was *knocked out* in the first round.

______________ **11.** The gangster was *knocked off* by his own men.

______________ **12.** Someone *knocked over* the liquor store last night.

CHOOSING APPROPRIATE SYNONYMS

Most of us unconsciously adjust our level of language in certain situations. For example, a supervisor in an office might write an official report indicating that a certain employee had failed to "perform acceptably." To a co-worker, he might say that the person just couldn't "do the job." At home, however, he might confide to a relative that the employee just couldn't "hack it" or "cut the mustard."

The English language is particularly rich in **synonyms**—words or expressions that have the same or nearly the same meaning. The synonyms for a word may range from very formal to very informal. So in any given situation, a speaker or writer may have several words of varying appropriateness from which to choose. Just as a good dictionary can be some help in determining appropriate usage, it can also help in judging the appropriateness of a word. In the next chapter we will discuss another useful source of synonyms, the thesaurus. Choosing the most appropriate synonym more often requires developing a "feel" for the language. This comes only from careful reading, listening, and writing practice. You can practice your synonym skills in the following exercises.

EXERCISE 4: Arrange the words in each group of synonyms from the MOST FORMAL to the LEAST FORMAL by writing the proper letters in the columns to the right. The first one has been done for you.

	Most Formal	*Standard*	*Least Formal*
1. a. split **b.** left **c.** departed	c	b	a
2. a. sad **b.** dejected **c.** down in the dumps			
3. a. wealthy **b.** rich **c.** loaded			
4. a. lively **b.** animated **c.** up			
5. a. uptight **b.** tense **c.** anxious			
6. a. dig **b.** understand **c.** comprehend			
7. a. money **b.** dough **c.** funding			
8. a. fan **b.** enthusiast **c.** freak			
9. a. position **b.** job **c.** gig			
10. a. procrastinate **b.** put off **c.** delay			
11. a. exhausted **b.** tired **c.** wiped out			
12. a. drunk **b.** plastered **c.** intoxicated			

EXERCISE 5: The writer of the following letter to the editor has included 15 slang words or expressions that are inappropriate to the serious tone of his letter. Cross out the inappropriate usages and replace each one with an equivalent word or expression from the list that follows at the top of page 16.

To the editor:

It burns me up the way some people beef every time public employees ask for a raise. Why do they expect us to bite the bullet when we are being ripped off by this city? It boggles my mind that some people who have it made dare to shoot off their mouths on this issue when they have no idea what it's like to have their backs up against the wall. It's time for someone to tell it like it is.

The employees of this city shoulder heavy responsibilities in return for very little dough. Some of us are so hard up we can't support our families. Yet the city council gives the cold shoulder to every request we make for raises. They refuse to shell out a fair wage for a day's work. No way will we accept this attitude any longer. We will fight on until we are finally treated fair and square.

Yours truly,

Arthur Smith

Replacement List

endure patiently	treated unfairly
amazes me	express their opinion
makes me angry	be in desperate circumstances
are well-off	poor
present the facts	pay
ignores	We refuse to
money	justly
complain	

EXERCISE 6: Sandra Torrence is trying to impress her new boss by using what she thinks are impressive-sounding words in all her memos. What she doesn't know is that her boss is nicknamed "Short and Sweet Sidney" because he'll only read memos that use clear, unpretentious language. There are 15 excessively formal words or expressions in Sandra's memo. Cross out each one and replace it with a word or expression from the list that follows the memo and continues on page 17. Use your dictionary if you need to.

TO: Sidney Green

FROM: Sandra Torrence

At our last conclave several important subjects were canvassed. The discourse culminated in the following resolutions:

1) Compensation for part-time personnel cannot be augmented this year.

2) Annual salary increments are presently predicated on evaluations that are egregiously inequitable and must be modified.

3) Interdepartmental interface must be ameliorated as soon as possible.

Replacement List

employees	improved
decisions	changed
discussed	now

```
interaction between departments    discussion
based                              flagrantly unfair
wages                              resulted
meeting                            increased
yearly raises
```

OTHER KINDS OF APPROPRIATENESS

We don't all speak the same way, and we don't speak the same way about every topic. Why do we talk the way we do? And when are special kinds of language appropriate?

Regionalisms

Standard English is the accepted language level for educated persons throughout the United States. However, we all know that an educated speaker from Boston does not sound exactly like an educated speaker from New York. Similarly, we would expect a person who grew up in Chicago to use words quite differently from a person who grew up in a small town in Georgia. Not only do people from different parts of the country pronounce certain words differently, they also give different names to certain common objects and express certain relationships differently. These usages determined by geographic areas are referred to as **regionalisms.**

Many usage experts consider regionalisms colorful and would regret their absence. You should be aware of your own regionalisms, though, because some of them are considered substandard (the Southern expressions "might could" and "used to could," for example). Others may have to be "translated" when you're writing for an audience that includes readers from outside your own geographic area. The following exercise is designed to make you aware of your own regionalisms.

EXERCISE 7: Circle the letter of the word *you use most often* as the name for the object described. (**NOTE:** There are no "right" or "wrong" answers to this exercise.)

1. a flat breakfast cake made from batter poured onto a hot skillet

a. pancake **b.** flapjack **c.** battercake

2. a small body of flowing water not big enough to be a river

a. stream **b.** creek **c.** branch

3. a paper container

 a. bag b. sack c. poke

4. a container for carrying water

 a. pail b. bucket c. blickey

5. a piece of playground equipment consisting of a flat board anchored in the center with ends that move up and down

 a. seesaw b. teeter-totter c. teeterboard

6. small bumps that appear on the skin as a response to cold

 a. goose pimples b. goose flesh c. chill bumps

7. a heavy rain

 a. downpour b. pour-down c. drencher

8. a carbonated, non-alcoholic beverage

 a. soft drink b. soda c. pop

9. the hard central part of a cherry or peach

 a. pit b. stone c. seed

10. large insect with transparent, net-veined wings

 a. dragonfly b. mosquito hawk c. darning needle

Jargon

In addition to using a certain social level of language (formal, standard, informal, or substandard) and certain regionalisms, many Americans also use specialized vocabularies that relate to their jobs or special interests. Such a specialized vocabulary is known as **jargon.** Some jargon is necessary so that people with a specialized interest can communicate efficiently about technical aspects of their field. For example, if you own a personal computer, this excerpt from a computer magazine, if read in context, might tell you something you need to know:

> The programs outlined here are vanilla implementations that work under any version of DOS, including 2.10. They incorporate no optimization but merely illustrate file I/O concepts.
>
> *Micro Computing*, July 1984, p. 24

If you don't know much about computers, the excerpt may read like gibberish. And whenever anyone starts talking computer jargon, you may suddenly feel like an outsider. Like any other language habit, jargon not only communicates ideas, it also defines "insiders" and "outsiders."

Even the Wild West had its jargon. If you listened in confusion as a cowboy asked you whether you wanted some *axle grease* (food) and *belly wash* (coffee), to be followed by a *brain tablet* (cigarette), the *buckaroo* would spot you as a *tenderfoot* right away.

Critics complain that jargon often obscures instead of communicates ideas. You might argue, for example, that this explanation of "normal communication," written by a sociologist, doesn't communicate very well itself:

> In normal communication, an inter-subjectivity of mutual understanding, guaranteeing ego-identity, develops and is maintained . . .

Other critics charge that some experts intentionally use jargon to confuse the public or to cover up mistakes and wrong-doings. The following are some military terms adapted from the book *Jargon: How to Talk to Anyone About Anything**:

accidental delivery of ordnance equipment: unintentionally firing on your own troops
collateral damage: inadvertent destruction of innocent bystanders and their property
civilian irregular defense soldier: a mercenary soldier
OOPS: Occasionless Ordered Preemptive Strike; in other words, a nuclear war that begins by accident
pacification: a battle that is fought in the name of establishing peace

This kind of jargon overlaps with another variety of English, the euphemism (see page 20). A euphemism is a misleadingly pleasant term for an unpleasant reality.

Some jargon may become so familiar that it is used informally by people outside the specialized field in which it originated. For example, the term "hands-on" comes from computer jargon, but is now used to describe any kind of practical job-related training. Medical jargon, too—from *diagnosis, post-op,* and *IV* to "*hyper*" (short for *hyperactive*)—has become increasingly popular.

Jargon can be colorful and interesting, but using it excessively will make your writing hard to understand or limit your audience to those few readers "in the know." To communicate ideas simply and clearly, it is wise to avoid jargon whenever possible.

*Joel Homer, *Jargon: How to Talk to Anyone About Anything*. New York: Times Books, 1979.

EXERCISE 8: The jargon used by politicians and bureaucrats to confuse the public has been called *bafflegab*. Read the following paragraph written in bafflegab. Use the Glossary that follows to translate it. Then rewrite the paragraph in your own words. (**NOTE:** The "translations" in this glossary were prepared by someone with a good sense of humor.)

Because of a shortfall in our budget projections, I have temporarily precluded the idea of a tax cut this year. I am acting with all deliberate speed to set up a task force whose suggestions will be taken under advisement. Later, I will exercise options recommended by my staff. I am confident that such measures will bring interest rates down to acceptable levels and reassure those who, in the past, have perceived a credibility gap in my administration.

Glossary

acceptable levels: a level a politician can get away with without being hurt politically
to be confident: desperately hope
credibility gap: the public's perception that someone is not telling the whole truth
exercise options recommended by my staff: make a decision that can be blamed on somebody else
reassure: fool
shortfall: mistakenly high estimate
take under advisement: will probably ignore
temporarily preclude: decide against
with all deliberate speed: as slowly as I possibly can

Euphemisms

Sometimes the search for an appropriate synonym leads people to select words that are pleasant and unthreatening rather than blunt and explicit. These pleasant or neutral terms for unpleasant realities are called **euphemisms.** For example, many people try to soften the impact of talking about death by referring to it as "expiring" or "passing away." They may describe a drunk person as being "under the influence." And when they speak of venereal diseases, they refer to them as "social diseases."

Television commercials are full of euphemisms, especially those referring to bodily functions. People in commercials don't sweat; they *perspire*. Instead of being constipated, they suffer from *occasional irregularity*. They don't have toilets; they have *bathroom bowls*.

Opinions differ about the value of euphemisms. Some people see them as attempts to hide from unpleasant realities we are afraid to face or embarrassed to talk about. Changing the name of an unpleasant reality, they say, won't make it go away, but may make it easier for us to talk about the problem, or perhaps to ignore it entirely.

It's true that euphemisms can be used to minimize or conceal the truth. When car dealers refer to their merchandise as *preowned* rather than *used* or *secondhand,* they're trying to change the way people think of their product. When generals refer to retreats as *redeployments,* they're attempting to conceal the hard facts of the matter. And when nuclear strategists substitute the harmless phrase *expecting rain* for *all-out nuclear attack,* one wonders how their language may affect their plans and responses to a dangerous possibility.

On the other hand, some so-called euphemisms play a valuable role in changing our attitudes and perspectives. Referring to old people as *senior citizens* or to retarded children as *exceptional* or *special* gives a higher status to people whose rights and problems deserve more attention. And although we may smile at the term *sanitation engineer,* we can probably understand why a garbage collector might want a job title that conferred a little more dignity. Let those who deplore the euphemisms of our own day reflect on those of a century ago. Then, women were *in a family way* for nine months before their *confinement,* and even pianos stood on *limbs.*

Be aware of euphemisms and think carefully before you use them. Are you choosing a pale, comfortable word instead of a strong, vigorous one? Are you minimizing the truth of a difficult situation by covering it up with a "nice" word? Are you avoiding offending some people? Or are you protecting people's privacy or helping restore their dignity and respect by "renaming" them?

EXERCISE 9: Each word listed below is a euphemism for something considered embarrassing, unpleasant, or undignified. "Translate" each euphemism into blunter language.

1. expectorate ______________

2. powder room ______________

3. bathroom tissue ______________

4. dentures ______________

5. mortician ______________

6. memorial park ______________

7. facial blemish ______________

8. adult (movie, bookstore, language) ______________

Nonsexist Language

The growing use of nonsexist language reflects changing social realities as well as new standards of appropriateness. Linguistic equality is provided when terminology becomes more inclusive, and words do not make unnecessary distinctions between males and females. Gender should be as irrelevant in job titles as it has now become on the jobs themselves.

It makes little sense to refer to a woman as a mail*man*, a sales*man*, a fire*man*, or repair*man*. But substituting *-woman* for *-man* to mean females in these occupations only emphasizes the sex of the person doing the job. Use of a nonsexist job title emphasizes the function performed. Just as national law now forbids employment discrimination on the basis of sex, so should job titles be expressed in words that include both men and women. It should be pointed out also that the use of nonsexist job titles protects men who are entering traditionally female occupations (flight attendant) as much as it protects women entering formerly predominantly male occupations (manager). When a good nonsexist term such as *poet, lawyer,* or *doctor* already exists, use it. Terms such as *poetess, lady lawyer,* or *woman doctor* are unnecessary and condescending. The following table presents some modern job titles:

NONSEXIST JOB TITLES

INSTEAD OF SAYING:	SAY:
mailman	mail carrier, letter carrier
salesman	sales representative
fireman	firefighter
repairman	repairer, repair technician
policeman	police officer
businessman	business executive, manager, owner
foreman	operations supervisor, front-line supervisor
boatman	boat operator
lumberman	logger
watchman	guard
craftsman	artisan, crafts worker
steward, stewardess	flight attendant
congressman	member of Congress, legislative representative
clergyman	member of the clergy
deliveryman	delivery worker
cameraman	photographer, camera operator
gal Friday	general office assistant

Revised job titles are a solution to only one of the issues raised by the traditional sexist bias in our language. Another is the use of the word *man* to designate humanity in general. Here are some suggestions for avoiding this problem.

Don't say:	*When you mean*:
man, mankind	humanity, human beings, human race, people
manmade	artificial, synthetic, manufactured, of human origin
manpower	workers, workforce, personnel, staff
man-hours	work hours

Many traditional terms and popular expressions are demeaning and condescending to women. Here are some, along with suggestions for improvement:

Don't say:	*When you mean*:
the fair sex, the weaker sex, girls or ladies	women
the little woman, his better half	wife
sweet young thing	young woman, girl
career girl or woman	attorney, doctor, editor, business executive, etc.
"my girl"	my secretary, my assistant
co-ed	student

EXERCISE 10: Rewrite the following sentences, changing any sexist language.

1. My little woman just got a job as a mailman.
2. In man, childbirth occurs approximately nine months after conception.
3. The lady lawyer gave her closing statement.
4. I told my children to look for a policeman if they are ever lost.
5. Plastic is a manmade material.
6. On the average, the weaker sex lives longer than men.
7. I went to lunch with the girls at the office.
8. Alice and Harry are the two foremen on duty.

9. Citizens should write their congressmen about this important issue.
10. Mankind has yet to reach his potential.

Effective Communication

We are bombarded by messages every day, and we frequently must create important messages of our own. To communicate effectively and to understand the communications of others, we must be sensitive to the varieties of English. We must choose words that are appropriate to our intent and our audience. The kind of language we choose gives our speech and writing a certain tone that is just as important as the literal meanings of the words. Never use a word that might detract from the overall mood and impression you want to communicate.

EXERCISES FOR REVIEW

A. The italicized words in the sentences below are characteristic of differing language levels or varieties of English. Label the usages in each sentence as *formal, standard, informal, substandard, regionalism,* or *jargon*.

__________ **1.** It's hard to do your best work when you feel *pooped*.

__________ **2.** Who *brung* the potato salad?

__________ **3.** Sound engineers refer to the low-frequency irregularities produced by cassette playback heads as *head bumps*.

__________ **4.** *Abrogation* of existing programs will surely *exacerbate* the problem.

__________ **5.** *Canceling* existing programs will surely *make* the problem *worse*.

__________ **6.** Social scientists say our society is plagued with *anomie* and alienation.

__________ **7.** *Irregardless* of what anyone says, I *ain't* changing my mind.

__________ **8.** *Regardless* of what anyone says, I *am not* changing my mind.

__________ **9.** Even if I get *flack* for it, I'm going to *do my own thing*.

__________ **10.** I was fishing in the *branch* when a swarm of *mosquito hawks* appeared.

B. Match each informal expression in column A with its equivalent in standard English in column B.

		A		*B*
____	**1.**	freak out	**a.**	relatives
____	**2.**	wing it	**b.**	hurry
____	**3.**	kid	**c.**	improvise
____	**4.**	folks	**d.**	angry
____	**5.**	mad	**e.**	get excited, lose control
____	**6.**	hop to it	**f.**	enjoy
____	**7.**	lick (a problem)	**g.**	informer, contemptible person
____	**8.**	get a kick out of	**h.**	child
____	**9.**	fink	**i.**	exaggerated praise
____	**10.**	hype	**j.**	overcome

C. Arrange the words in each group of synonyms from the MOST FORMAL to the LEAST FORMAL by writing the proper letters in the columns to the right.

	Most Formal	*Standard*	*Least Formal*
1. a. hyperbolic **b.** exaggerated **c.** too much			
2. a. rip off **b.** larceny **c.** theft			
3. a. insane **b.** crazy **c.** bonkers			
4. a. poor **b.** impoverished **c.** hard up			
5. a. agitated **b.** shaken **c.** shook up			
6. a. terminated **b.** fired **c.** sacked			
7. a. question **b.** grill **c.** interrogate			

	Most Formal	*Standard*	*Least Formal*
8. **a.** affront **b.** insult **c.** put down			
9. **a.** drive up the wall **b.** infuriate **c.** make angry			
10. **a.** residence **b.** pad **c.** home			

D. Read each passage. If the writer has maintained an appropriate tone throughout the passage, write *consistent* in the blank. If the writer has not maintained an appropriate tone, write *inconsistent*. Then underline the words that are inappropriate.

________________ **1.** I contend that such practices violate the spirit of the law; in short, they stink. The citizens of our town should exercise their responsibility in this important matter and put the screws on local government until these unfair practices are changed.

________________ **2.** Children develop a sense of fair play when they are treated fairly by their parents. There is no doubt but what most parents really try hard to be fair. Nevertheless, if they have forgotten how the world looks through a child's eyes, they ain't going to achieve none of the objectives they desire.

________________ **3.** "I know this guy who's a real hotshot. I don't mean to put him down, but there's no way he's ever going to admit he's wrong, you know what I mean? Guys like that really drive me up the wall."

________________ **4.** A funny thing happened to me when I was a kid. I once overheard my mom say a certain person had "rocks in his head." For weeks I pondered the possible signification of such an anomalous condition. One day the man came to visit, and I stared at him all through dinner. Finally, I couldn't stand the suspense a moment longer. "Mom," I asked, in a voice loud enough for everyone to hear, "does that man *know* he has rocks in his head?"

________________ **5.** I have always been fascinated by astronomy. As a child, I gazed in wonder at the stars and listened with rapt attention to myths and legends about them. As I have grown older and learned the scientific explanations for astronomical phenomena, my wonder has only increased.

E. Translate each euphemism into blunter, more explicit language.

1. social disease ______________________
2. expecting rain ______________________
3. occasional irregularity ______________________
4. exceptional children ______________________
5. preowned ______________________
6. senior citizen ______________________
7. sanitation engineer ______________________
8. disadvantaged ______________________
9. redeployment ______________________
10. under the influence ______________________
11. pass away ______________________
12. perspire ______________________

F. Write a nonsexist term for each of the following.

1. repairman ______________________
2. the fair sex ______________________
3. mankind ______________________
4. salesman ______________________
5. fireman ______________________
6. stewardess ______________________
7. congressman ______________________
8. mailman ______________________
9. policeman ______________________
10. craftsman ______________________
11. manmade ______________________
12. his better half ______________________
13. man-hours ______________________
14. my girl (said by a boss) ______________________
15. manpower ______________________

3. FINDING A SYNONYM

The most ordinary words may have the most synonyms, or alternative ways of saying the same thing. Why *form* a house if you can *construct* or *design* it? Why *form* a plan if you can *devise* or *contrive* it? Why *form* a sculpture if you can *chisel* or *carve* it? It is just this abundance (superfluity, excessiveness, copiousness, profusion, bountiful quality) of our language that is its joy. Our synonyms are our linguistic wealth. Use them with abandon, freely and daringly, to color your speech. Use them cautiously, carefully, to be precise and advance your message.

DENOTATION AND CONNOTATION

Most synonyms are not completely interchangeable. As we saw in Chapter 2, some synonyms are more appropriate for formal occasions, while others are more appropriate for informal occasions. Furthermore, most synonyms do not have *exactly* the same meaning. They may have the same general meaning or *denotation,* but their *connotations*—the shades of meaning they suggest—may be quite different.

Consider the words *childish* and *childlike.* Both have the general meaning "like or characteristic of a child." *Childish,* however, is applied to a person who possesses the negative qualities of a child, immaturity and foolishness, while *childlike* is used to describe someone with the positive qualities of a child—innocence, frankness, and enthusiasm. There are many such pairs of synonyms, one with a favorable and one with an unfavorable connotation. Learning to distinguish between them can help you say what you mean—and understand accurately what you read and hear.

Some synonyms are simply more descriptive than others. For example, *capture, confiscate,* and *grab* are all more descriptive than their synonym *take.* Each has a distinct connotation that paints a vivid picture in the reader's mind. To make your writing more effective, always search for the more vivid, specific word, rather than being satisfied with a bland, general one.

Some synonyms express varying degrees of feeling or actions of varying forcefulness. To *request* something, for example, is not the same as to *demand* or *beg* for it, although all of these are synonyms for *ask*.

The distinctions among other synonyms can be quite subtle. Later in this chapter, for instance, you will find out that the words *shy, bashful, diffident, modest,* and *demure* all have slightly different connotations.

This chapter will train you to be sensitive to the kinds of distinctions described in the preceding paragraphs. Many of the synonyms you will study are words you will probably recognize, but whose limitations and implications you may not fully realize. By becoming more familiar with these synonyms and learning to use them precisely, you can substantially enrich your vocabulary. And by training yourself to search for vivid words, you will begin the process of becoming a better speaker and writer.

EXERCISE 1: Test your awareness of the connotations of 20 popular adjectives. In each pair, one synonym has a more favorable connotation than the other. Circle the word in each pair that you would rather have someone use to describe you.

1. plump/fat
2. cowardly/apprehensive
3. skinny/slender
4. cheap/thrifty
5. soft/flabby
6. thin-skinned/sensitive
7. carefree/careless
8. cold/neutral
9. kind/soft-hearted
10. firm/rigid

EXERCISE 2: The writer of the following paragraph has taken an exciting subject and made it boring through the use of "blah" words. The boring words are the ones that have been underlined. Look at the synonym list that follows the paragraph. Each item on the list is a specific, vivid word that could be used to replace one of the boring words or phrases in the story. Cross out the boring, "blah" words and write the appropriate vivid synonyms above them.

I had quite an interesting experience last week. As I was moving over some pretty big rocks at the base of some really steep, rocky areas, a violent storm came up suddenly. A strong, noisy wind pushed me to the ground, and a hard rain fell on my body. Getting to my feet, I went quickly to a nearby cave and went into it. Breathing fast and shallowly, I looked up at the sky. Suddenly, high above me, I saw a figure hanging from the cliffs and looking as if he were about to fall to the rocks below. A climber had lost his footing and slipped in the rain. He was desperately holding on to the rocks by his fingertips and trying to resist the wind with all his strength. From my nice safe place, I shook in fear and wondered what to do. Suddenly, the climber dropped to an overhanging place a few feet below him. Just as suddenly, the storm was over. The climber rested a minute and went on his way. Once my body stopped shaking, I too went on my way back home, admiring a courage I couldn't hope to be the equal of.

Replacement List

horror	pelted	cozy refuge
boulders	threw	a ledge
panting	scrambling	trembling
howling	sheer cliffs	clinging
adventure	fierce	shuddered
raced	ducked	match
spied	peered	fighting
dangling	plummet	

FINDING SYNONYMS: USING THE THESAURUS

Sometimes we realize that a word we're about to use is imprecise, too general, or just plain boring, but we can't think of another word to replace it. That's when a thesaurus can be helpful. A thesaurus is a dictionary of synonyms arranged in alphabetical order. Some words have their own individual entry in the thesaurus, while others are included under general categories. For example, if you look up the word *think* in *Roget's College Thesaurus*, you'll find the instructions "See THOUGHT." If you then look up the general category THOUGHT, you will find the following entry:

THOUGHT

Nouns—**1,** thought, thoughtfulness; reflection, cogitation, consideration, meditation, study, lucubration, speculation, deliberation, pondering; headwork, brainwork; cerebration; deep reflection, rumination, close study, application, ATTENTION; abstract thought, abstraction; contemplation, musing, preoccupation, brown study, reverie, Platonism; self-counsel, self-communing, self-consultation; association of ideas, succession of ideas, flow of ideas; train *or* current of thought.
2, afterthought, mature thought, reconsideration, second thought; retrospection; MEMORY; excogitation; examination (see INQUIRY); invention (see IMAGINATION).
3, IDEA; topic, subject of thought, material for thought; food for thought; subject, subject matter; matter, theme, thesis, text, business, affair, matter in hand, argument; motion, resolution; head, chapter; case, point; proposition, theorem; field of inquiry; moot point, problem.
Verbs—**1,** think, reflect, cogitate, cerebrate, excogitate, consider, deliberate, lucubrate; rationalize, speculate, contemplate, meditate, ponder, muse, dream, ruminate; brood upon; animadvert, study; bend *or* apply the mind; digest, discuss, weigh; realize, appreciate; fancy.
2, take into consideration; take counsel, commune with oneself, bethink oneself; collect one's thoughts; revolve, turn over *or* run over in the mind; sleep on; rack one's brains; set one's wits to work; puzzle over; take into one's head; bear in mind; reconsider. *Colloq.*, sweat over, chew the cud, mull over. *Slang*, kick around.
3, occur, present itself, suggest itself; come into one's head; strike one, cross the mind, occupy the mind; have on one's mind; make an impression; sink in, penetrate the mind; engross the thoughts.
Adjectives—thinking, thoughtful, pensive, meditative, reflective, musing, wistful, contemplative, speculative, deliberative, studious, sedate, introspective, Platonic, philosophical; rational; lost in thought, engrossed, absorbed, rapt, preoccupied; in the mind, under consideration.
Adverbs—thoughtfully, reflectively; all things considered.
Antonyms, see RASHNESS.

Notice that the entry includes synonyms for the noun *thought*, as well as the verb *think*, the adjective *thinking*, and the adverb *thoughtfully*. It also refers you to other entries ("see IMAGINATION," "see INQUIRY") that may be helpful.

The primary benefit of a thesaurus is to remind you of words you already know but may not be able to remember when you need them. It presents you with a wealth of interesting synonyms at various levels of language. (Notice the verbs in the excerpt that are labeled *Colloq.* or *Slang.*) The usefulness of a thesaurus is limited, though, as many students have discovered after casually selecting a synonym that turned out to be inexact or inappropriate. The thesaurus does not discuss distinctions between synonyms at all, and it does not give you examples of how the words should be used. For that kind of help, you need a good dictionary. Still, when a word you are already familiar with is "on the tip of your tongue," the thesaurus is probably the best resource you can use to find it fast.

EXERCISE 3: Look up the following verbs in a thesaurus and list at least ten synonyms for each one. If the thesaurus refers you to a general category, consult the verbs listed under that entry as well.

1. look (also see VISION):

2. walk (also see TRAVEL):

3. eat (also see FOOD):

4. fall (also see DESCENT):

5. love:

CHOOSING A SYNONYM: USING THE DICTIONARY

A good dictionary lists and defines synonyms at the end of many entries. It does not list as many synonyms as a thesaurus does, but it can help you figure out which synonym best communicates what you want to say in a given situation. In Exercise 3, for example, you found at least ten synonyms for the verb *look* in the thesaurus—but no guidance on how to use them. The excerpt below, taken from the entry for *look* in *Webster's New World Dictionary, Second College Edition,* lists only six synonyms, but it tells you exactly how each one should be used. Read the excerpt and then try Exercise 4.

> ***SYN.*—look** is the general term meaning to direct the eyes in order to see *[*don't *look* now*]*; **gaze** implies a looking intently and steadily, as in wonder, delight, or interest *[*to *gaze* at the stars*]*; to **stare** is to look fixedly with wide-open eyes, as in surprise, curiosity, abstraction, etc. *[*it is rude to *stare* at people*]*; to **gape** is to stare with the mouth open in ignorant or naive wonder or curiosity *[*the child stood *gaping* at the elephant*]*; to **glare** is to stare fiercely or angrily *[*he *glared* at her for talking*]*; to **peek** is to take a quick, furtive look, as through a hole or from behind a barrier, at something not supposed to be seen; to **peer** is to look searchingly with the eyes narrowed *[*she *peered* down the well*]* See also APPEARANCE

EXERCISE 4: Refer to the dictionary excerpt for *look* and fill in the best synonym for each blank. Each synonym should be used only once, so read all of the sentences before you begin filling in the blanks.

1. I like to ____________ fondly at my sweetheart.
2. Ted couldn't help but ____________ as the flying saucer landed in front of him.
3. Put your hands over your eyes and promise not to ____________.
4. ____________ at me when I talk to you!
5. We had to ____________ through the telescope for several minutes before we could sight the ship.
6. Whenever she ____________ at me that way, I know I've done something wrong.
7. When I'm thinking hard, I tend to ____________ into space.

The remainder of this chapter will use excerpts from *Webster's New World Dictionary, Second College Edition,* to guide you as you practice using synonyms to say exactly what you mean.

Curious, Inquisitive, Meddlesome, Prying

> ***SYN.*—curious,** in this comparison, implies eagerness or anxiousness to find out things and may suggest a wholesome desire to be informed; **inquisitive** implies a habitual tendency to be curious, esp. about matters that do not concern one, and an attempt to gain information by persistent questioning; **meddlesome** suggests unwelcome intrusion into the affairs of others; **prying** suggests an officious inquisitiveness and meddlesomeness that persist against resistance

Notice that *curious* is a general word that often has a favorable connotation. *Inquisitive,* on the other hand, has a slightly negative connotation, because it implies persistent questioning about something that may not be a person's legitimate concern. *Meddlesome* is more negative, suggesting "unwelcome intrusion." *Prying* is the most negative of the synonyms, suggesting meddling that is overbearing and that persists despite resistance.

Test your understanding of these synonyms by trying Exercise 5.

EXERCISE 5: Choose the best synonym for each sentence. Each synonym should be used only once.

1. The mother tried to discourage her __________ child from asking the guest too many personal questions.
2. I did not appreciate his __________ interest in my project.
3. One must be __________ in order to learn.
4. Despite our repeated complaints, our __________ relative will not stop interfering in our business.

Easy, Facile, Effortless, Smooth, Simple

> ***SYN.*—easy** is the broadest term here in its application to that which demands little effort or presents little difficulty *[easy work]*; **facile** means occurring, moving, working, etc. easily and quickly, sometimes unfavorably suggesting a lack of thoroughness or depth *[a facile style]*; **effortless,** in contrast, favorably suggests expert skill or knowledge as responsible for performance that seems to require no effort *[the effortless grace of the skater]*; **smooth** suggests freedom from or riddance of irregularities, obstacles, or difficulties as bringing ease of movement *[a smooth path to success]*; **simple,** in this connection, suggests freedom from complication, elaboration, or involvement, as making something easy to understand *[a simple explanation]* ***—ANT.* hard, difficult**

Notice that *easy* and *simple* are both general words, with no built-in judgments associated with them. *Easy* means "demanding little effort," and *simple* means "uncomplicated" or "easy to understand." *Facile,* however, is often used to criticize something that came *too* easily to a person, because he or she didn't investigate the subject enough to discover its complexities. *Effortless*, on the other hand, is used to praise a performance that only *looks* easy because the person doing it is so skilled. *Smooth*, too, may be used to describe a successful performance, but its focus is on the absence of obstacles or difficulties in the situation itself.

EXERCISE 6: Choose the best synonym for each sentence. Each synonym should be used only once.

1. The plan was ____________ but effective.
2. The singer's seemingly ____________ performance was a joy to experience.
3. Their objections should be ____________ to overcome.
4. Our flight to Tulsa was ____________ and uneventful.
5. He always has a ____________ explanation for complex problems.

Reveal, Disclose, Divulge, Tell, Betray

SYN.—**reveal** implies a making known of something hidden or secret, as if by drawing back a veil [to *reveal* one's identity]; **disclose** suggests a laying open, as to inspection, of what has previously been concealed [he refuses to *disclose* his intentions]; **divulge** suggests that what has been disclosed should properly have been kept secret or private [do not *divulge* the contents of this letter]; **tell** may also imply a breach of confidence [kiss and *tell*] but more commonly suggests the making known of necessary or requested information [*tell* me what to do]; **betray** implies either faithlessness in divulging something [*betrayed* by an informer] or inadvertence in revealing something [her blush *betrayed* embarrassment] —***ANT.*** **conceal, hide**

Notice that *reveal* and *disclose* are neutral words that do not pass judgment on the person who makes information known. They are often used interchangeably. *Tell* can either be neutral or imply a negative judgment, depending on how it is used. *Divulge* is always negative, implying that what is being made known should have been kept secret. *Betray* is usually the most negative of these synonyms, suggesting disloyalty. Betraying your country or someone's trust is a serious matter. But *betray* can also mean to reveal something unintentionally or against one's will. In that sense, betraying one's feelings is not necessarily such a serious matter.

EXERCISE 7: Choose the best synonym for each sentence. Each synonym should be used only once.

1. My trembling hands will ______________ my fear.
2. I promised not to ______________ the secret password.
3. ______________ her what they said.
4. The new study will ______________ some surprising facts.
5. The senator will ______________ the details of his campaign financing tomorrow.

Try the next two groups of synonyms on your own. Read the dictionary excerpts. Then complete Exercises 8 and 9.

Crowd, Throng, Multitude, Swarm, Mob, Host, Horde

SYN.—**crowd** is applied to an assembly of persons or things in close proximity or densely packed together and may suggest lack of order, loss of personal identity, etc. [*crowds* lined the street]; **throng** specifically suggests a moving crowd of people pushing one another [*throngs* of celebrators at Times Square]; **multitude** stresses greatness of number in referring to persons or things assembled or considered together [a *multitude* arrayed against him]; **swarm** suggests a large, continuously moving group [a *swarm* of sightseers]; **mob**, properly applied to a disorderly or lawless crowd, is an abusive term when used to describe the masses or any specific group of people; **host** specifically suggests a large organized body marshaled together but may be used generally of any sizable group considered collectively [he has a *host* of friends]; **horde** specifically refers to any large predatory band [a *horde* of office seekers]

EXERCISE 8: Refer to the preceding dictionary excerpt to answer the following questions.

1. Which two synonyms have the strongest negative connotations?
2. Which two synonyms specifically suggest a moving group of people?
3. Which synonym is often neutral, but may suggest loss of order or identity?
4. Which two synonyms merely suggest a large group?

Famous, Renowned, Celebrated, Noted, Notorious, Distinguished, Eminent, Illustrious

> ***SYN.*—famous** is applied to persons or things that have received wide public attention and are generally known and talked about; **renowned** suggests a being named publicly again and again for some outstanding quality, achievement, etc.; **celebrated** is applied to persons or things that have received much public honor or praise; **noted** implies a being brought to the wide notice of the public for some particular quality; **notorious**, in current usage, suggests a being widely but unfavorably known or talked about; **distinguished** implies a being noted as superior in its class or of its kind; **eminent** more strongly stresses the conspicuous superiority of persons or things; **illustrious** suggests a reputation based on brilliance of achievement or splendidness of character —***ANT.* obscure, unknown**

EXERCISE 9: Refer to the preceding dictionary excerpt to answer the following questions.

1. Which two synonyms simply suggest being well-known, without implying either a favorable or unfavorable connotation?
2. Which synonym has an unfavorable connotation?
3. Which word has a slightly more favorable connotation, *distinguished* or *eminent*?

Probable, Possible, Likely

> ***SYN.*—probable** applies to that which appears reasonable on the basis of evidence or logic but is neither certain nor proved; **possible** applies to that which, although not probable, can conceivably exist, occur, be done, etc.; **likely** suggests greater probability than **possible**, but less credibility than **probable** —***ANT.* improbable, unlikely**

A *possible* event is one that *could* happen. A *likely* event is one that has a good chance of happening. A *probable* event is one that is *expected* to happen.

A *possible* cause is one worth considering. A *likely* cause is one worth investigating. A *probable* cause is one supported by the evidence.

EXERCISE 10: Refer to the preceding dictionary excerpt to answer the following questions.

1. Barbara is a likely winner. Stu is a possible winner. Donna is the probable winner. Who would you bet your money on? __________

2. To convict a defendant, the prosecution must show ______________ cause for presuming the defendant's guilt.

Decline, Refuse, Reject, Repudiate, Spurn

SYN.*—decline** implies courtesy in expressing one's nonacceptance of an invitation, proposal, etc. *[he declined the nomination]*; **refuse** is a more direct, sometimes even blunt term, implying an emphatic denial of a request, demand, etc. *[to refuse a person money]*; **reject** stresses a negative or antagonistic attitude and implies positive refusal to accept, use, believe, etc. *[they rejected the damaged goods]*; **repudiate** implies the disowning, disavowal, or casting off with condemnation of a person or thing as having no authority, worth, validity, truth, etc. *[to repudiate the claims of faith healers]*; to **spurn** is to refuse or reject with contempt or disdain *[she spurned his attentions]* —ANT.* accept**

These synonyms provide a useful range of verbs to express our feelings about not accepting something. If we want to turn something down politely, we can *decline* it. If we want to be less polite, we can *refuse*. If we want to express a negative attitude toward the thing we are turning down, we can say we *reject* it. If we want to express an even stronger negative attitude, especially one of moral condemnation, we can *repudiate* something. If we want to express our feelings of contempt for the person making the offer, we can *spurn* it.

EXERCISE 11: Choose the best synonym for each sentence. Each synonym should be used only once.

1. He ______________ the evil ideas of totalitarian government.
2. I regret that I must ______________ your gracious invitation.
3. Quality control will ______________ this product because of its faulty workmanship.
4. Why does he ______________ to let us help?
5. They will ______________ his insincere, self-serving apology.

Try the last two groups of synonyms on your own. Read the dictionary excerpts. Then complete Exercises 12 and 13.

Try, Attempt, Endeavor, Essay, Strive, Struggle

SYN.—**try** is commonly the simple direct word for putting forth effort to do something [*try* to come], but specifically it connotes experimentation in testing or proving something [I'll *try* your recipe]; **attempt**, somewhat more formal, suggests a setting out to accomplish something but often connotes failure [he had *attempted* to take his life]; **endeavor** suggests exertion and determined effort in the face of difficulties [we shall *endeavor* to recover your loss]; **essay** connotes a tentative experimenting to test the feasibility of something difficult [he will not *essay* the high jump]; **strive** suggests great, earnest exertion to accomplish something [*strive* to win]; **struggle** suggests a violent striving to overcome obstacles or to free oneself from an impediment [he *struggled* to reach the top]

EXERCISE 12: Refer to the preceding dictionary excerpt to answer the following questions.

1. Which three synonyms specifically suggest exertion and determination?
2. Which of the synonyms you listed in question 1 implies the greatest exertion?
3. Which synonym often has a connotation of failure?
4. Which synonym suggests a preliminary, tentative effort?
5. Which synonym is a commonly used word for the general idea of "putting forth effort"?

Shy, Bashful, Diffident, Modest, Demure

SYN.—**shy** implies a shrinking from the notice of others and a reticence in approaching them, either as an inherent trait or as resulting from inexperience; **bashful** implies such shyness as is displayed in awkward behavior and embarrassed timidity; **diffident** implies a self-distrust and lack of self-confidence that makes one reluctant to assert oneself; **modest** implies an unassuming manner in one who, because of his ability, achievements, etc., might be expected to assert himself strongly; **demure**, in current usage, suggests a decorously modest manner, often one that is affectedly so —*ANT.* **bold, confident**

EXERCISE 13: Refer to the preceding dictionary excerpt to answer the following questions.

1. Which synonym specifically suggests awkwardness and embarrassment?
2. Which synonym seems to have the most favorable connotation?

3. Which synonym specifically suggests a lack of self-confidence?

4. Which synonym would you use to describe someone whose modesty seemed artificial?

EXERCISES FOR REVIEW

A.

I am *assertive.*
You are too *aggressive.*
He is *pushy.*

The above examples illustrate a game that demonstrates how we use "loaded" words to make ourselves look good and other people look bad. You play the game by attributing the most favorable characteristic to "I," a less favorable word to "you," and the least favorable word to "he." Try the game with some words you've studied in this unit.

1. inquisitive, curious, meddlesome

 a. I am __________ .

 b. You are __________ .

 c. He is __________ .

2. facile, easy, effortless

 a. My performance looked __________ .

 b. Your performance looked __________ .

 c. His performance was __________ .

3. disclose, divulge, betray

 a. I __________ the truth.

 b. You __________ a secret.

 c. He __________ a confidence.

4. multitude, mob, crowd

 a. I was one of the __________ .

 b. You were one of the __________ .

 c. He was one of the __________ .

5. distinguished, notorious, noted

a. I am a ______________ author.

b. You are a ______________ author.

c. He is a ______________ author.

6. likely, probable, possible

a. I am the ______________ winner.

b. You are a ______________ winner.

c. He is a ______________ winner.

7. gaze, look, gape

a. I ______________ in wonder at the awesome sight.

b. You ______________ at it.

c. He ______________ in ignorant disbelief.

8. decline, spurn, refuse

a. I graciously ______________ offers of assistance.

b. You ______________ to let anyone help you.

c. He ______________ everyone who tries to help him.

B. Look up the verb *give* in a thesaurus and list as many synonyms as you can find.

***SYN.*—give** is the general word meaning to transfer from one's own possession to that of another; **grant** implies that there has been a request or an expressed desire for the thing given [to *grant* a favor]; **present** implies a certain formality in the giving and often connotes considerable value in the gift [he *presented* the school with a library]; **donate** is used especially of a giving to some philanthropic or religious cause; **bestow** stresses that the thing is given gratuitously and often implies condescension in the giver [to *bestow* charity upon the poor]; **confer** implies that the giver is a superior and that the thing given is an honor, privilege, etc. [to *confer* a title, a college degree, etc.]

C. Use the preceding dictionary excerpt to fill in the blanks with the best synonyms. Each synonym should be used only once.

1. I will ______________ your wish on one condition.

2. We always ______________ used clothing to the church rummage sales.

3. ______________ her the book.

4. Only the queen can ______________ the title of lord.

5. We will ______________ the award tomorrow at an official ceremony.

6. The homecoming queen ______________ her smiles upon the crowd.

D. Read the following dictionary excerpt and then fill in each blank below with the best synonym. Each synonym should be used only once.

> *SYN.*—**show** implies a putting or bringing something into view so that it can be seen or looked at [*show* us the garden]; to **display** something is to spread it out before one so that it is shown to advantage [jewelry *displayed* on a sales counter]; **exhibit** implies prominent display, often for the purpose of attracting public attention or inspection [to *exhibit* products at an exposition]; **expose** implies the laying open and displaying of something that has been covered or concealed [this bathing suit *exposes* her scar]; **flaunt** implies an ostentatious, impudent, or defiant display [to *flaunt* one's riches, vices, etc.]

1. A journalist might ______________ a scandal.

2. A museum might ______________ artifacts.

3. A store owner might ______________ his merchandise.

4. Wealthy people might ______________ their minks and diamonds.

5. You might ______________ me your wedding pictures.

4. HOMONYMS AND OTHER CONFUSING WORDS

In Chapters 2 and 3 you learned how to use synonyms—words with nearly the same meaning—to express yourself appropriately, precisely, and colorfully.

In this chapter you will study *homonyms* and other confusing words. Homonyms are words that sound alike but are spelled differently and have different meanings (*knight* and *night*, for example). Other words may sound similar and be confusing for that reason (*advice* and *advise*, for example). If you are careless about synonyms your writing will be vague, colorless, or unclear in meaning. But it could still be understood. If, however, you misuse homonyms your writing may actually say something that is entirely different from what you mean. For example, a *complementary* remark is totally different from a *complimentary* one. Furthermore, a matter of *principle* is not at all the same as a matter of *principal*. And it makes a big difference whether you describe a witness as *credible* or *credulous*.

Mastering these confusing sound-alikes is one area of vocabulary study that requires memorization and practice. This chapter serves two purposes. First, it's an alphabetical glossary of confusing words, so you can quickly look up words of which you're unsure. At the same time, it's a series of lessons, with exercises presented every few pages, so that you can test your understanding as you go along. The review exercises at the end of the chapter will measure how much you've learned and make you aware of those words to which you should devote further study.

HOMONYMS

aisle—passageway between rows of seats
isle—small island

EXAMPLES: The movie fans rushed down the *aisle* to their seats.
We explored a beautiful *isle* in the Caribbean.

aloud—in an audible voice, out loud
allowed—permitted

EXAMPLES: I read the letter *aloud* to my mother.
Their children are not *allowed* to stay up late.

altar—table used for religious ceremonies
alter—to change, adjust

EXAMPLES: The priest stood before the *altar*.
It's too late to *alter* our course.

bare—(1) without clothes or covering (2) to uncover
bear—(1) the animal (2) to withstand or endure (3) to carry (4) to produce

EXAMPLES: By November, most of the trees were *bare*.
The lion *bared* his teeth.
The *bear* climbed the tree.
I can't *bear* to watch.
She must *bear* the burden alone.
That peach tree will soon *bear* fruit.

berth—sleeping place
birth—act of being born

EXAMPLES: I chose to sleep in the lower *berth*.
The proud parents announced the *birth* of their child.

board—(1) piece of wood (2) governing body, council
bored—(1) made someone weary by being dull (2) made a hole by drilling

EXAMPLES: Use that *board* to make a shelf.
The *board* of directors meets on Friday.
That play *bored* me.
They *bored* a hole through the wall.

born—given birth to
borne—past participle of *to bear*, meaning (1) carried (2) produced

EXAMPLES: He was *born* in 1965.
The seeds were *borne* by the wind.

brake—device used to slow down or stop a vehicle
break—(1) to smash, split into pieces (2) to stop working

EXAMPLES: Our *brakes* failed on the mountain road.
Be careful not to *break* that vase.

bridal—relating to a bride or wedding
bridle—(1) harness (2) to restrain

EXAMPLES: The *bridal* party is rehearsing for the wedding.
Do you know how to put the *bridle* on the horse?
His *unbridled* greed was his downfall.

capital—(1) city in which a state or national government is located (2) involving or punishable by death (3) money or property
capitol—(1) [C-] the building in which the United States Congress meets (2) [c-] building in which a state legislature meets

EXAMPLES: Washington, D.C., is the *capital* of the United States.
Do you support the idea of *capital* punishment?
How much *capital* do we need to start a business?
The U.S. *Capitol* is famous for its beautiful dome.
Boston's state house *capitol* dome is covered in gold leaf.

carat—unit of weight for precious stones
caret—a mark (^) used to indicate where something should be added to a line of writing
carrot—the vegetable

EXAMPLES: The bracelet was made of 18-*carat* gold.
Place a *caret* where you wish to add the words.
Carrots are a good source of vitamin A.

cent—coin that equals 1/100 of a dollar
scent—smell
sent—past tense of to send
sense—intelligence, logic, judgment

EXAMPLES: The candy bar costs forty *cents*.
The *scent* of honeysuckle was in the air.
He *sent* the package by express mail.
His explanation didn't make any *sense*.

cereal—breakfast food
serial—(1) of or in a series (2) story or film presented in successive parts

EXAMPLES: She likes fruit with her *cereal*.
Every typewriter in the office has its own *serial* number.

cite—to name
sight—(1) something seen (2) ability to see (3) to observe, look carefully
site—location

EXAMPLES: Can you *cite* an example to prove your point?
Niagara Falls is a spectacular *sight*.
Even when she was ninety her *sight* was excellent.
From the tower we were able to *sight* the winding river.
This land will be the *site* of the new school.

coarse—(1) rough (2) unrefined, not in good taste
course—(1) direction, path, series of events (2) part of a meal (3) unit of instruction

EXAMPLES: Holding on to the *coarse* rope hurt my hands.
His *coarse* remark was uncalled for.
The captain changed the ship's *course*.
Do you think you can pass this *course*?
We had soup as our first *course*.

EXERCISE 1: Underline the correct word in each sentence.

1. No one is (aloud/allowed) to enter the theater after the play begins.
2. Her (bare/bear) shoulders were sunburned.
3. The bus was so crowded that people were standing in the (aisles/isles).
4. The building where Congress meets is called the (Capital/Capitol).
5. You looked (board/bored) in class yesterday.
6. The suit must be (altared/altered) before it will fit him.
7. She can't (bare/bear) the suspense a moment longer.
8. Can the (coarse/course) of true love ever run smoothly?
9. Read the poem (aloud/allowed) to us.
10. Were you (born/borne) in Cincinnati?
11. Can Wilson (brake/break) the world's record this year?
12. The school (board/bored) will vote tomorrow.
13. Do you want to sleep in the upper (berth/birth)?
14. Pump the (brakes/breaks) to avoid skidding.
15. The horse's (bridal/bridle) didn't fit well.
16. They were stranded on a desert (aisle/isle).
17. The (altar/alter) was covered with a white cloth.
18. Tallahassee is the (capital/capitol) of Florida.
19. I love (carat/caret/carrot) cake.
20. The editor placed a (carat/caret/carrot) where the words were to be inserted.
21. Someone once pointed out that common (cents/sense) is not really very common.

22. That case was (cited/sighted/sited) as an example of unfair practices.

23. The dam will be built on this (cite/sight/site).

24. A secret admirer (cent/scent/sent) her a valentine.

25. Do you have a copy of your (berth/birth) certificate?

26. That tree has not (born/borne) much fruit this year.

27. The ring contained a 20- (carat/caret/carrot) diamond.

28. What flowers is she carrying in her (bridal/bridle) bouquet?

29. I have only fifteen (cents/scents/sense) in my wallet.

30. He lost his (cite/sight/site) in an accident.

31. Radio soap operas used to be known as (cereals/serials).

32. The (coarse/course) fabric did not feel pleasant next to my skin.

33. Whole-grain (cereal/serial) is a good source of fiber.

complement—(1) that which completes (2) to make complete
compliment—praise

EXAMPLES: The yellow dahlias *complement* the color scheme of the room.
She *complimented* him on his speech.

complementary—(1) completing, balancing (often used to describe a relationship in which each member makes up for what the other lacks)
complimentary—(1) expressing praise (2) free

EXAMPLES: The two women worked well together because their skills were *complementary*.
The speaker's remarks about television were not very *complimentary*.
We received *complimentary* tickets to the concert.

core—center
corps—organized group

EXAMPLES: Throw away the apple *core*.
He joined the Marine *Corps*.

council—an advisory or governing group
counsel—(1) advice (2) to advise

EXAMPLES: There are two new members of the town *council*.
He *counseled* his friend to be careful.

desert (dez′ ərt)—dry, barren, sandy area
desert (di zurt′)—to abandon
dessert (di zurt′)—a sweet course served at the end of a meal

EXAMPLES: He was lost in the *desert* for ten days.
Why did the soldier *desert* his post?
We had apple pie for *dessert*.

die—(1) to stop living (*-ing* form is *dying*) (2) singular of *dice*
dye—to color (*-ing* form is *dyeing*)

EXAMPLES: The patient may *die*. The patient is *dying*.
There is only one *die* in Trivial Pursuit.
They will *dye* the cloth red. They are *dyeing* the cloth.

dual—pertaining to two, having two parts or kinds.
duel—combat between two persons

EXAMPLES: His invention was a *dual*-purpose machine.
They chose their weapons and began the *duel*.

fair—(1) festival or carnival (2) clear and sunny (3) light-colored, blond (4) just
fare—(1) money paid for transportation (2) food (3) get along, succeed

EXAMPLES: Dan won a stuffed animal at the *fair*.
The weather will be *fair* and warm.
I have *fair* skin.
The judge made a *fair* decision.
We paid our *fare* and found a seat on the bus.
The *fare* at camp was simple but nutritious.
How did you *fare* at the income tax inquiry?

flair—natural talent, sense of style
flare—(1) to blaze up (2) to burst out in anger (3) to curve outward (4) bright light used as a distress signal

EXAMPLES: He has a *flair* for creative writing.
The fire *flared* suddenly.
She *flared* up at the question.
She was wearing a *flared* skirt.
He set out a *flare* while he changed the tire.

forth—forward, onward
fourth—4th

EXAMPLES: A witness came *forth* to testify.
He was the *fourth* person in line.

gorilla—the animal
guerrilla—small defensive force of irregular soldiers, usually volunteers, making surprise raids, especially behind the lines of an invading enemy army (2) the type of warfare carried on by this type of force

EXAMPLES: We like to watch the *gorillas* at the zoo.
Many revolutions depend on *guerrilla* forces.

grate—(1) to grind, rub, or scrape into particles (2) to irritate
great—much above ordinary in size, quality, nobility, or importance

EXAMPLES: Help me to *grate* these carrots.
Loud radios *grate* on my nerves.
He was a *great* help to me.

hail—(1) frozen raindrops (2) to summon, call out, welcome, greet
hale—healthy

EXAMPLES: We *hailed* a taxi at the corner.
My grandfather is still *hale* and active.

hear—to perceive sounds
here—in this place

EXAMPLES: Did you *hear* someone cough?
Come *here* right now!

EXERCISE 2: Underline the correct word in each sentence.

1. Jack was elected to the student (council/counsel).
2. She received many (complements/compliments) on her performance.
3. What's for (desert/dessert)?
4. This plant looks as if it's about to (die/dye). What can I do to prevent it from (dying/dyeing)?
5. It isn't (fair/fare) to demand special privileges.
6. The (core/corps) of the earth is made of molten metal.
7. How much is the train (fair/fare) to Pittsburgh?
8. (Hear/Here) is the money that I owe you.
9. He looks very (hail/hale) for his age.
10. I need to (great/grate) a cup of cheese for this recipe.
11. United States troops fought against (gorilla/guerrilla) forces in Vietnam.
12. No one has come (forth/fourth) with an explanation.

13. Tempers (flaired/flared) during the difficult negotiations.

14. Aaron Burr killed Alexander Hamilton in a (dual/duel).

15. It is amazing how many creatures can survive in the (desert/dessert).

16. I want to (die/dye) this dress blue. Do you know anything about (dying/dyeing) clothes?

17. He is a member of our diplomatic (core/corps) in Paris.

18. My stereo has (dual/duel) controls.

19. He has a (flair/flare) for the dramatic.

20. She won (forth/fourth) prize in the race.

21. The restaurant served a (complementary/complimentary) cocktail with every meal.

22. Good friends often have (complementary/complimentary) strengths and personalities.

23. The old man's good (council/counsel) was an invaluable help to his grandson.

24. Don't (desert/dessert) us now!

25. Can you (hear/here) what the speaker is saying?

26. His ideas (complement/compliment) mine; together we can write a comprehensive report.

27. The (gorilla/guerrilla) is the largest and most powerful of the apes.

28. Who do you think was our (gratest/greatest) president?

29. It began to (hail/hale) during the thunderstorm.

idle—(1) unemployed, inactive (2) lazy (3) worthless or unfounded
idol—(1) image of a god used as an object of worship (2) a person who is strongly or excessively admired

EXAMPLES: The *idle* men still hoped to find jobs.
I spent an *idle* summer at home.
That charge is based on *idle* rumors.
The golden *idol* was stolen from the shrine.
Martina Navratilova is the young tennis player's *idol*.

knew—past tense of *know*
new—opposite of old

EXAMPLES: I *knew* that would happen.
We need some *new* members.

know—to be aware, understand, recognize
no—opposite of yes; not any

EXAMPLES: Who *knows* the answer?
The answer is *no*.
There is *no* reason to despair.

lie—(1) to recline (2) to make a false statement
lye—a strong alkaline substance

EXAMPLES: *Lie* down and take a nap.
Don't *lie* to the police.
The *lye* burned a hole in the cloth.

morn—poetic word for morning
mourn—to lament, grieve, feel sorrow

EXAMPLES: It was a pleasant and delightful midsummer's *morn*.
We *mourned* the death of a great leader.

our—belonging to us
hour—60 minutes

EXAMPLES: *Our* house needs to be painted.
The program is an *hour* long.

pail—bucket
pale—colorless or light in color

EXAMPLES: Fill this *pail* with water.
He looked *pale* after his illness.

pain—sensation of hurt, discomfort, or distress
pane—sheet of glass

EXAMPLES: He suffered *pain* in his lower back.
The window *pane* was broken.

peace—absence of war or disturbance
piece—(1) part or fragment (2) a single thing

EXAMPLES: The *peace* treaty was signed last week.
The child asked for a *piece* of candy.

plain—(1) clear, open (2) not fancy or complicated, ordinary (3) an extent of level country
plane—(1) flat surface (2) two-dimensional (3) to make smooth or level (4) clipped form of *airplane*

EXAMPLES: The house stood in *plain* view.
Her dress was very *plain*.
Settlers crossed the Great *Plains*.
The carpenter *planed* the wood.

pore—(1) a small opening (2) to study intently
pour—(1) to cause to flow (2) to rain heavily

EXAMPLES: Sweat seeps through *pores* in the skin.
He was *poring* over the morning newspaper, looking for news of the accident.
Pour him a glass of milk.

pray—to say a prayer; beg
prey—(1) animal hunted for food by another animal (2) to plunder or swindle (3) to weigh heavily

EXAMPLES: The priest *prayed* for peace.
The lion stalked its *prey*.
The muggers *preyed* on the elderly.
Feelings of guilt *preyed* on his mind.

principal—(1) first in rank, authority, or importance; main (2) head of a school (3) amount of an investment or bank deposit, or of a debt minus interest
principle—fundamental truth, law, or belief

EXAMPLES: Apathy was the *principal* cause of our defeat.
Who is the new high school *principal*?
Her investment was so successful that the interest soon equaled the *principal*!
She refused to compromise her moral *principles*.

real—actual, true, authentic, sincere
reel—(1) spool on which film or line is wound (2) a lively dance (3) to sway or stagger, feel dizzy

EXAMPLES: This chair is a *real* antique.
Bring your rod and *reel*, and we'll go fishing.
One well-known American folk dance is the Virginia *reel*.
The fighter was *reeling* from the blow.

right—(1) opposite of wrong (2) opposite of left (3) that which a person has a just claim to
rite—ceremony
write—to compose, put down words to be read

EXAMPLES: Did you know the *right* answer?
Turn *right* at the corner.
He works for the Civil *Rights* Commission.
The anthropologist described the tribe's marriage *rites*.
Did he *write* that best-selling novel?

EXERCISE 3: Underline the correct word in each sentence.

1. His (knew/new) address is 45 Water Street.
2. I (know/no) what you mean.
3. The workers were (idle/idol) all morning while the machinery was being repaired.
4. They (die/dye) eggs for Easter.
5. I sat in the waiting room for an (our/hour).
6. His shirt was (pail/pale) yellow.
7. The widow experienced a period of deep (morning/mourning).
8. Bring me a mop and a (pail/pale) of hot water.
9. It's (plain/plane) that the witnesses (lie/lye).
10. A (peace/piece) of the puzzle was missing.
11. It is (poring/pouring) outside.
12. She was arrested for disturbing the (peace/piece).
13. We washed all the window (pains/panes).
14. (Plain/Plane) geometry is the study of two-dimensional figures.
15. The ruthless swindler (prayed/preyed) on the weak and helpless.
16. It is your (right/rite) to call your attorney.
17. The projectionist showed the (reals/reels) of film in the wrong order.
18. (Rite/Write) to me while you're away.
19. We studied the basic (principals/principles) of philosophy.
20. His concern for you is (real/reel).
21. She (prays/preys) for their safe return.
22. That actress is my (idle/idol).
23. There is (know/no) doubt of the outcome.
24. We (knew/new) you'd be there.
25. Soap used to be made from (lie/lye).
26. He rode out alone that fateful (morn/mourn).
27. The bad news caused them much (pain/pane).

28. The treatment was supposed to cleanse the (pores/pours) of her face.

29. His (principal/principle) reason for coming is to see you.

30. A ceremony in which a young person is recognized as an adult is called a (rite/right) of passage.

role—(1) part played by an actor or by a person in a real-life situation
roll—(1) to turn over and over (2) list of names for checking attendance (3) small bread or cake

EXAMPLES: Who played the *role* of Hamlet?
What was your *role* in the negotiations?
The children *rolled* down the hill.
The teacher called the *roll.*
I like sweet *rolls* for breakfast.

seen—past participle of *see*
scene—(1) part of a play (2) place where an event occurs (3) display of strong feelings in front of others

EXAMPLES: Have you *seen* his latest movie?
The wedding took place in the last *scene.*
The governor visited the *scene* of the disaster.
Some late-arriving guests made a *scene.*

shone—past tense and past participle of *shine*
shown—past participle of *show*

EXAMPLES: The sun *shone* through my window.
You have *shown* considerable progress.

soar—to fly
sore—painful

EXAMPLES: We watched the hawk *soar* through the sky.
The pitcher's arm was *sore* after the big game.

sole—(1) only, lone (2) kind of fish
soul—spirit

EXAMPLES: He was the *sole* survivor of the crash.
I bought *sole* for dinner.
Many religions teach that human beings have a *soul* as well as a body.

stake—(1) pointed object that is driven into the ground (2) something risked in a game or contest (3) share or interest in a venture
steak—slice of meat

EXAMPLES: We can't set up the tent until the *stakes* are in place.
What is at *stake* in this election?
His life savings were his *stake* in the silver mine.
How do you like your *steak* cooked?

stationary—fixed, unmoving
stationery—paper and envelopes used for writing letters

EXAMPLES: Some of the parts are movable; others are *stationary*.
All his memos are written on official company *stationery*.

steal—to take something that belongs to another
steel—a hard metal

EXAMPLES: Did someone *steal* your bicycle?
Many kitchen utensils are made of stainless *steel*.

threw—past tense of *throw*
through—(1) in one side and out the other (2) finished

EXAMPLES: The pitcher *threw* a fastball.
We drive *through* the tunnel.
Are you *through* with that book?

throne—the chair on which a king or queen sits
thrown—past participle of *throw*

EXAMPLES: The ancient *throne* was made of gold.
The pitcher has *thrown* several fastballs.

waist—part of the body between the ribs and the hips
waste—(1) to use up or spend needlessly (2) left over, no longer useful

EXAMPLES: The slacks were too small in the *waist*.
Don't *waste* your money on that.
The *waste* food was taken by the poor people.

ware(s)—merchandise
wear—(1) to have on the body (2) to cause to deteriorate by use
where—at what place

EXAMPLES: The merchant displayed his *wares*.
What are you going to *wear* to the party?
The car showed signs of *wear* before the year was over.
Where are you going?

weak—opposite of strong
week—seven days

EXAMPLES: The patient felt *weak* after his surgery.
Your pictures will be ready in a *week*.

weather—atmospheric conditions
whether—if

EXAMPLES: The *weather* report predicted rain.
I don't know *whether* I can attend.

EXERCISE 4: Underline the correct word in each sentence.

1. The actors rehearsed the second (seen/scene) of the play.
2. The full moon (shone/shown) brightly that night.
3. She was the (sole/soul) heir to the huge fortune.
4. His fate was decided by a (role/roll) of the dice.
5. We cooked some (stakes/steaks) on the grill.
6. My friend likes to write on pretty (stationary/stationery).
7. My muscles are (soar/sore) from exercising.
8. Do you have a big (stake/steak) in the outcome?
9. Call her back next (weak/week).
10. Most people would like to lose a few inches around the (waist/waste).
11. How should a boomerang be (throne/thrown)?
12. Her friends (threw/through) a shower for her.
13. (Wear/Where) did you buy that?
14. Do you know (weather/whether) it's supposed to rain?
15. She won an Academy Award for her (role/roll) in that movie.
16. Now I've (seen/scene) everything!
17. Our car is so old that no one would want to (steal/steel) it.
18. Have they (shone/shown) you the pictures of their vacation?
19. I can't decide what to (wear/where).
20. The (weather/whether) has been very changeable lately.
21. The salesman showed us his (wares/wears).

22. He put his heart and (sole/soul) into the project.
23. Our spirits (soared/sored) when we heard the good news.
24. A (stationary/stationery) front is one that is not moving.
25. (Steal/Steel) is known for its strength.

OTHER CONFUSING WORDS

The words in the following confusing pairs do not sound exactly alike, but their spelling and pronunciation are similar enough that people tend to misuse them. Read the list and check off any pairs that you tend to misuse. Try to remember the example sentences for each pair or make up example sentences of your own that are easy to remember. After you have studied the list carefully, try Exercise 5.

advice—(noun) opinion given as to what to do
advise—(verb) to give advice

EXAMPLES: I asked her for *advice*.
She *advised* me to take the job.

affect—to cause, to have an effect on
effect—(verb) to make, do, or accomplish; (noun) a result or an influence

EXAMPLES: Will the hurricane forecast *affect* your vacation plans?
It could *effect* a change in our route.
It will have the *effect* of delaying our departure.

continually—refers to repeated, interrupted action
continuously—refers to uninterrupted action

EXAMPLES: He *continually* demands my attention.
The machine has run *continuously* for twelve hours.

credible—believable (refers to the thing that is believed)
credulous—too easily convinced, too ready to believe (refers to the person who believes)

EXAMPLES: The suspect gave a *credible* account of his actions.
Credulous persons tend to believe everything they read.

emigrate—to leave a country
immigrate—to come to a country

EXAMPLES: They *emigrated* from Poland.
They *immigrated* to the United States.

flaunt—to display something proudly or defiantly
flout—to show contempt for; mock; scorn

EXAMPLES: He *flaunted* his wealth in front of the less fortunate.
The outlaw *flouted* the laws of society.

incredible—unbelievable
incredulous—unwilling or unable to believe, skeptical

EXAMPLES: She found my story *incredible.*
She was *incredulous* when she heard my story.

ingenious—clever, inventive, original
ingenuous—frank, open, naive

EXAMPLES: He has an *ingenious* idea for a new product.
He had an *ingenuous* manner that was rare for someone in the business world.

later—comparative form of *late*
latter—refers to the second-mentioned of two items, as opposed to *former*, which refers to the first-mentioned of two items

EXAMPLES: It's *later* than you think.
John and Henry are my friends. The former is an engineer; the *latter* is an accountant.

loose—(1) opposite of tight (2) free, unconfined
lose—(1) to become unable to find (2) opposite of win

EXAMPLES: The child's tooth is *loose.*
We turned the animal *loose.*
Please don't *lose* the key.
I always *lose* at poker.

moral—(1) having to do with right and wrong (2) good, virtuous (3) lesson taught by a fable, event, etc.
morale—emotional condition

EXAMPLES: He lived according to strong *moral* principles.
The *morale* of the team was low.

personal—pertaining to a person, private
personnel—a group of people employed in the same service

EXAMPLES: I have *personal* reasons for my request.
All *personnel* are entitled to health insurance benefits.

persecute—to cause to suffer unjustly
prosecute—to proceed against by law

EXAMPLES: No one should be *persecuted* because of his color or creed.
All offenders will be *prosecuted* to the full extent of the law.

prescribe—(1) to designate as a remedy (2) to set down rules, order
proscribe—to forbid

EXAMPLES: The doctor *prescribed* medication for the patient.
Some activities are *proscribed* by the rules; others are merely discouraged.

respectfully—with respect
respectively—refers back to each of several things in the order that they were mentioned

EXAMPLES: He treated his parents *respectfully*.
Jane and Alice contributed food and clothing, *respectively*. (Jane contributed food; Alice contributed clothing.)

EXERCISE 5: Underline the correct word in each sentence.

1. The telephone rang (continually/continuously) all day.
2. You must learn to be more skeptical instead of being so (credible/credulous).
3. Will they be allowed to (emigrate/immigrate) from the Soviet Union?
4. His (advice/advise) was simple: "Don't go."
5. Leaders who (flaunt/flout) their power make many enemies.
6. Leaders who (flaunt/flout) the law can be subject to legal (persecution/prosecution).
7. Low (moral/morale) among our office (personal/personnel) is causing a decline in productivity.
8. Her (ingenious/ingenuous), childlike behavior was refreshing.
9. It's (incredible/incredulous) that he could have survived.
10. The former is my boss; the (later/latter) is my assistant.
11. This knot is coming (loose/lose).
12. The flight arrived (later/latter) than we'd expected.
13. We have a close (personal/personnel) relationship.

14. What is the (moral/morale) of the story?
15. I can't (advice/advise) you any further.
16. The flame has been burning (continually/continuously) for hours.
17. Thousands of people (emigrate/immigrate) to the United States each year.
18. They had a (credible/credulous) explanation for their behavior.
19. She was disappointed to (loose/lose) the race.
20. She came up with an (ingenious/ingenuous) solution to a problem that had at first seemed unsolvable.
21. I was (incredible/incredulous) when I heard about their plan to clean up the environment.
22. The gold and silver medals went to the United States and Czechoslovakia (respectfully/respectively).
23. The prisoner was (persecuted/prosecuted) unmercifully by the guards.
24. I must (respectfully/respectively) disagree.
25. What (affect/effect) was the decorator trying for in that room?
26. The sad story of her childhood (affected/effected) everyone who heard it.

EXERCISES FOR REVIEW

A. The writer of the following editorial has misused 15 homonyms and other confusing words. Cross out each incorrect form and write the correct form above it.

I knew are plan to regulate businesses in this city would ultimately succeed. It was plane to me, however, that the president of the city counsel would have to play a major role in getting the bill passed. Now that it has, it will be sited as an important precedent for other cities across the nation. Already we have received complementary letters from leaders in our nation's capital.

Experience has shone that hear in our city promises are not worth the stationary they are written on. What counts is action. I respectfully suggest that it is the morale responsibility of our leaders to protect us from unprincipaled swindlers who pray on the poor and the weak. It is our rite to expect this kind of protection. Weather the mayor likes this responsibility or not, it is one he must accept if he does not want to loose the respect of the average citizen. It seems incredible that he has aloud dishonest men to openly flout the law for so long.

B. You don't often see two homonyms used together, but it's fun to imagine situations in which you might. A certain animal without clothes on might be called a *bare bear*, for example. A tasteless, unrefined series of lectures might be called a *coarse course*. Try to identify the other "doubles" described below. Each answer is a pair of homonyms listed below.

1. an unemployed, admired person: an ____________ ____________

2. sixty minutes belonging to us: ____________ ____________

3. an authentic spool: a ____________ ____________

4. the correct ceremony: the ____________ ____________

5. the only spirit: the ____________ ____________

6. to abandon the last course of a meal: to ____________ ____________

7. a just amount of money to pay for a trip: a ____________ ____________

8. a light-colored bucket: a ____________ ____________

9. a flying vehicle that is not fancy: a ____________ ____________

10. the main rule or law: the ____________ ____________

11. writing paper that does not move: ____________ ____________

12. a seven-day period that lacks strength: a ____________ ____________

Word List

desert	pail	rite
dessert	pale	right
fair	plain	sole
fare	plane	soul
hour	principal	stationery
our	principle	stationary
idol	reel	weak
idle	real	week

5. TROUBLE-SHOOTING FOR GOOD SPELLING

Book One of MASTERING VOCABULARY devotes a chapter to the spelling rules that apply to English words (when to use *ie* and when to use *ei*, when to double a final consonant, etc.). These rules are useful, and you may want to review them before beginning this spelling enrichment chapter.

Unfortunately, though, knowing the rules is not enough. Being a good speller requires a "trouble-shooting" approach to words. A trouble-shooter is an expert who is called in on a job to identify a problem and fix it. Good spellers are trouble-shooters because they pay attention to the words they encounter in their everyday reading. They look the words over and study how they're put together. They may even "take a picture" of the words in their minds. They are always on the lookout for certain spelling "trouble spots," such as silent letters, double letters, or schwa sounds that occur often in English words. They make a mental note of such trouble spots as they read, so that when the time comes to use a certain word in their writing they are already on familiar terms with it.

This chapter will give you practice in becoming a spelling trouble-shooter. The first part of the chapter will show you certain troublesome spelling patterns in English words and help you find ways of remembering some words that contain those patterns. In the second part of the chapter you will apply your trouble-shooting skills as you learn the spelling and meaning of words from six specialized fields: government and politics, food and cookery, health and medicine, business and finance, law, and the arts.

In this chapter you will find many words to study and many chances to test your spelling of problem words. As you read through the word lists and do the exercises, check those words that give you trouble. Enter them on page 83 to make your own list of spelling problems, and study them carefully before doing the review exercises at the end of the chapter.

PRONOUNCE IT CAREFULLY—SPELL IT RIGHT

Many spelling errors result from pronunciation errors. For example, some people misspell the word *strictly* because they fail to pronounce the final *t* in the word. Many people misspell the word *mischievous* (mis′ čhi vəs) because they mispronounce it, consequently adding an extra syllable—and an extra letter—to the word. Sometimes mispronouncing a word causes people to reverse the order of certain letters in the word. For example, many people misspell the word *hundred* (hun′ drid) because they mispronounce it "hun′ dərd."

The following lists present some words that are often misspelled because they are mispronounced. The trouble spot in each word is underlined. Study these "troublemakers" by pronouncing each word aloud carefully. Then copy the correct spelling of the word in the blank. Make sure you have not added, left out, or reversed letters. Put a check mark next to each word whose spelling is hard for you to remember. Take extra time to practice pronouncing and spelling those words. Then try Exercise 1.

Don't add extra letters to:

athletic (ath let′ ik) ____________________

disastrous (di zas′ trəs) ____________________

drowned (dround) ____________________

hindrance (hin′ drəns) ____________________

height (hīt) ____________________

Don't leave out letters from:

boundary (boun′ drē) ____________________

different (dif′ ər ənt) ____________________

environment (in vī′ rən mənt) ____________________

February (feb′ rə wer′ ē) ____________________

government (guv′ ər mənt) ____________________

miniature (min′ ē ə chər) ____________________

probably (präb′ ə blē) ____________________

quantity (kwän′ tə tē) ____________________

recognize (rek′ əg nīz′) ____________________

several (sev′ ər əl) ____________________

surprise (sər prīz′) ____________________

temperature (tem′ prə chər) ____________________

privilege (priv′ ′l ij) ____________________

library (lī′ brer ē) ____________________

Don't reverse letters in:

children (chil′ drən) ____________________

hundred (hun′ drid) ____________________

perspiration (pur′ spə rā′ shən) ____________________

perform (pər fôrm′) ____________________

EXERCISE 1: Circle the correctly spelled word in each pair. When you have finished the exercise, check your work by referring to the word list on pages 62 and 63.

1. hindrance, hinderance
2. different, diffrent
3. children, childern
4. height, heighth
5. goverment, government
6. preform, perform (to act)
7. quanaty, quantity
8. surprise, supprise
9. drownded, drowned
10. February, Febuary
11. prespiration, perspiration
12. minature, miniature
13. probly, probably
14. hundred, hunderd
15. privlege, privilege
16. boundary, boundry
17. environment, enviernment
18. temperture, temperature
19. atheletic, athletic
20. disastrous, disasterous
21. sevral, several
22. recognize, recanize

SILENT LETTERS

Good pronunciation can help you spell some words but not others. That's because many English words contain letters that are not pronounced. The following list contains examples of words with silent letters. Notice that some of the words represent a pattern common to a whole group of words (the silent *t* in *fasten*, for example).

Study the word list by reading it carefully and making a mental note of the silent letter (or letters) in each word. Copy the correct spelling of the word in the blank. Then try Exercise 2.

Remember the silent letters in these words:

business ____________________

condemn ____________________
(also solemn, hymn, column)

exhibit ____________________
(also exhilarate)

fasten ____________________
(also whistle, wrestle, listen, etc.)

fiery ____________________

parliament ____________________

psychology ____________________
(also psychic, psychiatry)

resign ____________________
(also assign, benign, etc.)

stalk ____________________
(also walk, folk, chalk, etc.)

through ____________________
(also though, weigh, fight, etc.)

EXERCISE 2: Circle the correctly spelled word in each pair. Refer to the above list to check your work.

1. exibit, exhibit
2. fassen, fasten
3. parliament, parlament
4. psychology, psycology
5. resine, resign
6. busness, business
7. condemn, condem
8. firey, fiery
9. throu, through
10. stalk, stauk

DOUBLE LETTERS

Words with double letters can confuse even the best spellers, especially since some words have one pair of double letters, some have two pairs, and a very few even have three. (Memorize the two examples listed in this section: *committee* and *bookkeeper*. They're the most common.)

After you've memorized the spelling of the first two words on the list, take your time with numbers 3 through 10. Look carefully at each word that contains two pairs of double letters. Try to "take a picture" of each word in your mind. Pronounce the word and tell yourself to remember each set of double letters. Then write the word in the blank and check your spelling carefully. Place a check mark next to any word whose spelling is difficult for you to remember. Then move on to the third group and repeat the process. When you feel ready, try Exercise 3.

These words contain three pairs of double letters:

committee ______________________

bookkeeper ______________________

These words contain two pairs of double letters:

accommodate ______________________

address ______________________

aggressive ______________________

assassin ______________________

commission ______________________

embarrass ______________________

occurrence ______________________

possession ______________________

These words contain one pair of double letters:

accumulate ______________________

disappoint ______________________

exaggerate ______________________

excellent ______________________

innocence ______________________

necessary ______________________

occasional ______________________

omission ______________________

parallel ______________________

tomorrow ______________________

EXERCISE 3: Circle the correctly spelled word in each pair. Check your answers.

1. dissapoint, disappoint
2. address, adress
3. comittee, committee
4. parallel, parralel
5. comission, commission
6. omission, ommission
7. accommodate, accomodate
8. aggressive, agressive
9. exaggerate, exagerate
10. tommorow, tomorrow
11. occurrence, occurence
12. excellent, excelent
13. embarass, embarrass
14. assasin, assassin
15. possession, posession
16. innocence, inocence
17. accummulate, accumulate
18. neccessary, necessary
19. occasional, occassional
20. bookkeeper, bookeeper

THE SCHWA SOUND

Many English words contain the "uh" sound (also known as the schwa sound) in an unaccented syllable. Unfortunately for spelling, that "uh" sound is represented by different vowels in different words. Many spellers mistakenly rely on the letter *a* to represent this sound. Keep in mind that, except for words ending in *able* and *ant*, most commonly misspelled words use *e*, *i*, or *o*, rather than *a*, to represent the schwa sound. Study the following examples, and write them in the spaces provided. Then try Exercise 4.

In these words, the "uh" sound is represented by e:

academy
benefited
category
mathematics
phenomenon

In these words, the "uh" sound is represented by i:

authority
definitely

medicine ______________________________

optimism ______________________________

responsibility ______________________________

In these words, the "uh" sound is represented by o:

alcohol ______________________________

monotonous ______________________________

controversy ______________________________

philosophy ______________________________

apologize ______________________________

EXERCISE 4: Circle the correctly spelled word in each pair. Check your work.

1. benefited, benifited
2. defanitely, definitely
3. authoraty, authority
4. academy, acadamy
5. controversy, contraversy
6. alcahol, alcohol
7. medecine, medicine
8. mathamatics, mathematics
9. apologize, apolagize
10. optamism, optimism
11. phenomenon, phenomonon
12. philosiphy, philosophy
13. catagory, category
14. monotonous, monotanous
15. responsability, responsibility

CONFUSING BEGINNINGS: *DE* OR *DI*

The letters *de* and *di* often have a similar sound when they occur in the unaccented first syllable of words. That's why some spellers have trouble remembering which words begin with *de* and which begin with *di*. If you have trouble with the following two lists, you may want to pronounce the *de* sound "dē" and the *di* sound "dī" as you study the words. Pronouncing the sounds differently for spelling purposes will help you remember when to use *de* and when to use *di*. Study the lists on page 68. Then try Exercise 5, which can be found on pages 68 and 69.

Some "de" Words:

debase
debate
decay
decease
deceive, deception
decide, decision
declare, declaration
decline, declension
deduct
deface
defeat
default
defect, defective
defend, defendant
defer (to put off)
deform
defrost
degrade
delectable
deliberate
delicate, delicacy
delight
deliver
delude, delusion
demand
demented
denote
depend
depose
describe, description
despair, desperation
detect
device (noun)
devise (verb)

Some "di" Words:

dichotomy
differ (to have another opinion)
diffuse, diffusion
digest
dilate
dilemma
diligent, diligence
dilute
dimension
diminish, diminution
diploma
direct, direction
dirigible
disability
disadvantage
disaster
discard
disease
dispel
dispense
dispose, disposable
display
dissolve
distract
divert
divide, division

EXERCISE 5: Circle the correctly spelled word in each pair. Check your work.

1. dispel, despel
2. dimand, demand
3. desplay, display
4. dicision, decision

5. divise, devise
6. description, discription
7. devide, divide
8. desease, disease
9. device, divice
10. derect, direct
11. dicay, decay
12. diliver, deliver
13. degest, digest
14. dissolve, dessolve
15. diform, deform
16. dilude, delude
17. dicline, decline
18. deduct, diduct
19. delight, dilight
20. deminish, diminish

CONFUSING ENDINGS: *ABLE* AND *IBLE*

Certain word endings can cause spellers headaches too. Many of us have trouble remembering whether certain words end in *ant* or *ent*, *er* or *or*. Words ending in *able* and *ible* trip up even many professional writers and editors. One way to remember how to spell these words is to pronounce the endings differently as you study the words. Pronounce the *ible* ending "ĭ b'l" and the *able* ending "ā b'l" as you read down the lists. Then "take a picture" of each word with your eyes, focusing on the troublesome ending. Copy the words in the blanks. When you're ready, try Exercise 6.

These words end in *able*:

depend<u>able</u> ____________________

indispens<u>able</u> ____________________

inevit<u>able</u> ____________________

irrit<u>able</u> ____________________

predict<u>able</u> ____________________

These words end in *ible*:

compat<u>ible</u> ____________________

irresist<u>ible</u> ____________________

poss<u>ible</u> ____________________

suscept<u>ible</u> ____________________

vis<u>ible</u> ____________________

EXERCISE 6: Circle the correctly spelled word in each pair. Check your work.

1. inevitable, inevitible
2. irresistible, irresistable
3. compatable, compatible
4. irritable, irritible
5. predictible, predictable
6. indispensable, indispensible
7. dependable, dependible
8. possable, possible
9. susceptable, susceptible
10. visable, visible

BE A TROUBLE-SHOOTER AS YOU READ AND WRITE

In this chapter so far you have been practicing your spelling skills with words having six kinds of trouble spots. Careful spellers should train their eyes and ears to notice and remember them. For each kind of spelling problem, of course, there are many more examples than have been included here. Train yourself to pronounce words carefully as an aid to spelling. In your reading, be on the lookout for silent letters and double letters in words and make a mental note of them. Notice which letter is used to make the "uh" sound in various words. Exaggerate the pronunciations of confusing word beginnings and word endings to help you remember them.

Be aware of spelling trouble spots in your own writing, too. Do you often misspell words that use the letters *sc* for the *s* sound (fa*sc*inate, *sc*issors, adole*sc*ent, etc.) or words that use *ch* for the *k* sound (*ch*aos, s*ch*edule, me*ch*anic, *ch*aracter, etc.)? Keep a list of your own spelling "demons" and refer to it before submitting any written work. Consult the list as you check, or proofread, your work for spelling errors.

The remainder of this chapter is a combination vocabulary/spelling program that will familiarize you with the specialized vocabularies of government and politics, food and cooking, health and medicine, business and finance, law, and the arts. Each word list contains terms commonly used in a certain field—words which you are likely to find in your everyday reading or in certain special situations.

You will need access to a college dictionary to complete the exercises in this section. If you don't own a college dictionary, you may want to work on this section in a library. Your school or neighborhood library should contain several college dictionaries. After you look up the definitions of a group of words and study their spelling, you will complete exercises that involve "playing" with the words in word games and observe how the words are used in sentences. As you complete the exercises, you will become familiar with not only the spellings but also the meanings of the words. You'll also have a chance to put your trouble-shooting skills to work. As in the first part of this chapter, certain spelling trouble spots in the words are highlighted in italics. Study these trouble spots carefully and look for your own as well.

Government and Politics

This list contains words used to describe different kinds of governments and political people, issues, and processes. Look up the spelling and pronunciation of each word in a college dictionary. Write the pronunciation and definition next to the word. Study how the words are spelled, paying close attention to trouble spots. You may want to pay extra attention to the French terms *coup d'état* and *laissez-faire*. When you feel familiar with these words, try Exercises 7, 8, and 9.

ambassador ____

____

bureaucracy ____

____

candidate ____

____

consensus ____

____

constitutional ____

____

coup d'état ____

____

delegates ____

____

democracy

fascism

government

ideology

judiciary

laissez-faire

legislature

majority

monarchy

representative

parliament

totalitarian

EXERCISE 7: Underline the correctly spelled word in each pair.

1. Did any of the (canadates/candidates) receive a (majority/majoratory) of the votes?
2. Did the (delagates/delegates) to the convention reach a (concensus/consensus) on the issues?
3. The (judishiary/judiciary) is the branch of government that decides whether laws are (constitutional/constatutional).
4. The (ambassader/ambassador) reported to the embassy.
5. People in a (totalatarien/totalitarian) society have few rights.

EXERCISE 8: The words defined below are taken from the Government and Politics word list. Fill in the correctly spelled word that fits each definition. Refer to the list on pages 71 and 72 if you need help. Then transfer the letters from the blanks numbered 1–8 to complete this quotation:

QUOTATION: "I don't belong to any organized political party.

I'm a ___ ___ ___ ___ ___ ___ ___ ___."
(1 2 3 4 5 6 7 8)

DEFINITIONS:

1. type of dictatorship characterized by central control of economy and militaristic policies

   f ___ ___ ___ ___ ___ ___ ___ (5 under the 4th blank)

2. the departments and officials that carry out government activities

   b ___ ___ ___ ___ ___ ___ ___ ___ ___ ___ (2 under the 4th blank)

3. rule by the people

   d ___ ___ ___ ___ ___ ___ ___ ___ (3 under the 3rd blank)

4. sudden overthrow of a government by force (2 words)

   c ___ ___ ___ ___ ' ___ ___ ___ ___ (1 under the 5th blank)

5. set of political beliefs

i__ ___ ___ ___ ___ ___ ___ ___
(4)

6. policy of letting business and industry do as they please (2 words)

l__ ___ ___ ___ ___ ___ ___
(7)

f__ ___ ___ ___ ___
(6)

7. an elected member of a legislature

r__ ___ ___ ___ ___ ___ ___ ___ ___ ___ ___ ___ ___ ___
(8)

Food and Cooking

Many of the words on this list are probably so familiar to you that you won't need to look them up in the dictionary. Nonetheless, they are all tricky to spell. Pay close attention to the underlined trouble spots. Devote extra practice to the many French (*bouillon, soufflé, sauté,* etc.) and Italian (*cappuccino, lasagne,* etc.) words on the list.

appetizer	dessert
barbecue	hors d'oeuvres
biscuit	lasagne
bouillon	margarine
broccoli	mayonnaise
cantaloupe	mozzarella
cappuccino	omelet *or* omelette
casserole	quiche
chili	raspberry
chocolate	recipe
cinnamon	sauté
cocoa	soufflé
coffee	spaghetti
croissant	vegetable
cuisine	vinaigrette
culinary	yogurt
decaffeinated	zucchini

EXERCISE 9: Correct the spelling errors in the following menu.

MENU

Breakfast

Omlets: Your choice of cheddar or mozarella cheese. Served with bagel, biscits, or croissant.

Lunch

Each entree comes with your choice of vegtable.

Barbaqued spare ribs

Chilli con carne

Spinach quiche

Dinner

Each entree comes with appetizer and your choice of vegtable.

Spagetti

Lasagne

Brocolli and zucchini casarole

Salads

Fresh garden salad with your choice of mayonaise or vinagrette dressing.

Deserts

Choclate Dream Cake

Frozen yogurt with your choice of fruit topping: strawberries, razberries, or cantalope.

Beverages

Orange juice

Milk

Decaffenated coffee

Cappucino with cinammon

EXERCISE 10: The words defined below are taken from the Food and Cooking word list. Fill in the correctly spelled word that fits each definition. Refer to the list on page 74 if you need help. The letters in the numbered blanks will spell out a word that means "a person who enjoys and has a discriminating taste for foods":

___ ___ ___ ___ ___ ___ ___ ___ ___ ___
1 2 3 4 5 6 7 8 9 10

DEFINITIONS:

a. a food made from fermented milk

y ___ ___ ___ ___ ___
(blank 6 = 4)

b. a light and puffy baked dish, usually containing eggs and cheese

s ___ ___ ___ ___ ___ ___
(blank 2 = 6)

c. a solidified vegetable oil used in place of butter

m ___ ___ ___ ___ ___ ___ ___ ___
(blank 1 = 9; blank 4 = 1; blank 5 = 2)

d. a clear broth, usually of beef

b ___ ___ ___ ___ ___ ___ ___
(blank 2 = 8; blank 8 = 7)

e. another word for appetizers

h ___ ___ ___ ___ ' ___ ___ ___ ___ ___ ___ ___
(blank 4 = 3; blank 7 = 10; blank 10 = 5)

Health and Medicine

Look up the definition and pronunciation of any word with which you are not familiar. Write them next to the word. Then try to memorize the spelling of each word, concentrating on the "trouble spots."

aerobic	gynecologist
anatomy	hemorrhage
anesthesia	hypodermic
antihistamine	hypertension
appendectomy	hypochondriac
barbiturate	inoculation

bronchitis	migraine
carcinogen	neurological
cardiovascular	obstetrician
cartilage	ophthalmologist
chiropractor	paralysis
cholesterol	pediatrician
chromosome	penicillin
cirrhosis	pneumonia
congenital	schizophrenia
diarrhea	tonsils
eczema	tonsillectomy

EXERCISE 11: Cross out the misspelled word in each sentence. Then spell the word correctly in the blank at the end of the sentence.

1. Aerobic exercise is good for a person's cardio-vasculer system.

   ____

2. A low colesterol diet has been shown to reduce one's risk of developing hypertension. ____________________

3. Antihistamines and barbituates are two types of drugs.

   ____

4. Innoculations are given with a hypodermic needle. ____________

5. Diarrea is a symptom of many diseases. ____________________

6. He was born with a congenitle illness that resulted in paralysis.

   ____

7. Does he really suffer from exema and migraine headaches, or is he just a hypochondriac? ____________________

8. Bone and cartilage are important structures in the human anatamy.

   ____

9. The doctor administered penicilin to fight the patient's infection.

   ____

10. Medical researchers are studying the way that carcinagens attack our chromosomes. ____________________

EXERCISE 12: The words defined below are taken from the Health and Medicine word list. Each definition describes a certain medical specialist. Fill in the correctly spelled word that fits each definition. Refer to the word list on pages 76 and 77 if you need help. The letters in the numbered blanks will spell out the word for a specialist in the origin and history of words:

___	___	___	___	___	___	___	___	___	___	___
1	2	3	4	5	6	7	8	9	10	11

DEFINITIONS:

1. doctor who specializes in functions and diseases specific to women

g ___ ___ ___ ___ ___ ___ ___ ___ ___ ___ ___
(blank 2: 3; blank 4: 1; blank 9: 8)

2. doctor who specializes in pregnancy and childbirth

o ___ ___ ___ ___ ___ ___ ___ ___ ___ ___ ___
(blank 4: 11)

3. specialist, not an M.D., in manipulating joints, especially the spine

c ___ ___ ___ ___ ___ ___ ___ ___ ___ ___ ___
(blank 5: 7; blank 11: 5)

4. doctor who specializes in functions and diseases of the eye

o ___ ___ ___ ___ ___ ___ ___ ___ ___ ___ ___ ___ ___ ___
(blank 8: 4; blank 10: 6; blank 14: 10)

5. doctor who specializes in treating children

p ___ ___ ___ ___ ___ ___ ___ ___ ___ ___ ___
(blank 4: 9; blank 6: 2)

Business and Finance

Look up the definition and pronunciation of any word with which you are not familiar. Write them next to the word. Then try to memorize the spelling of each word, concentrating on the "trouble spots."

accrue
amortize
annuity
arrears
bankruptcy
capital

interest
lien
merchandise
mortgage
negotiable
personnel

collateral	principal
creditor	promissory note
depreciation	proprietor
entrepreneur	receipt

EXERCISE 13: One word in each of the following sentences is misspelled. Cross out the misspelled word and write it correctly.

1. How much intrest has accrued on your account?
2. The morgage was amortized over twenty-five years.
3. The crediter put a lien on her property.
4. The entrepreneur had enough capitol to start her own business.
5. He put up the merchandise in his store as colateral for a loan.

EXERCISE 14: The words defined below are taken from the Business and Finance word list. Fill in the correctly spelled word that fits each definition. Refer to the word list on pages 78 and 79 if you need help. The letters in the numbered blanks will spell out another word from the Business and Finance list:

___	___	___	___	___	___	___	___
1	2	3	4	5	6	7	8

DEFINITIONS:

1. one who owns and operates a business

p ___ ___ ___ ___ ___ ___ ___(6) ___(3) ___ ___

2. condition of being legally declared unable to pay one's debts

b ___ ___ ___ ___ ___ ___ ___(8) ___ ___

3. amount of a debt minus finance charges

p ___(5) ___ ___ ___ ___ ___ ___ ___

4. decrease in value of property

d ___ ___ ___ ___ ___ ___(1) ___ ___ ___ ___ ___(2)

5. written promise to pay a certain person on a certain date (2 words)

p ___ ___ ___ ___ ___ ___ ___ ___ ___
7

n ___ ___ ___
4

Law

Look up the definition and pronunciation of any word with which you are not familiar. Write them next to the word. Then try to memorize the spelling of each word, concentrating on the "trouble spots."

adjudicate	indictment
affidavit	jurisdiction
appellate court	larceny
arraign	misdemeanor
bail	negligence
circuit court	perjury
contract clause	plaintiff
copyright	plea bargain
defendant	prosecutor
felony	subpoena
homicide	writ

EXERCISE 15: Each sentence contains one misspelled word. Cross out the misspelled word and write it correctly.

1. The defendent was charged with two felonies: homicide and larceny.
2. After the suspect was arraigned, the judge handed down an inditement.
3. The prosecutor accused the witness of perjery.
4. Do copyrite violations fall within the jurisdiction of this court?
5. The lawyer delivered the papers requested in the subpoena and presented several other affadavits pertinent to the negligence case.
6. The misdemeanor will be ajudicated next week.

The Arts

Look up the definition and pronunciation of any word with which you are not familiar. Write them next to the word. Then try to memorize the spelling of each word, concentrating on the "trouble spots."

arabesques
autobiography
avant-garde
baroque
characterization
choreography
cinema
classic
climactic
connoisseur
crescendo
denouement
dramatist
fresco
genre
hyperbole
literati
memoir
metaphor
museum
protagonist
renaissance
rhyme
rhythm
scenario
sculptor
simile
soliloquy
staccato
surrealism
tragedy
villain
whimsy

EXERCISE 16: Twenty of the words from the Arts vocabulary list have been scrambled below. Unscramble each word and write it in the blank spaces below each definition. The definitions will give you an extra clue to the identity of each word. When you have filled in all the blanks, write down all the circled letters, in order, in the spaces at the end of the puzzle. These letters will spell out a quotation from the novelist Henry James about art. The A's are filled in to get you started.

1. a bad or evil character in a story or play: LILIVAN

(__) __ __ __ __ __ (__)

2. a figure of speech in which one object is used to suggest another: HORPMATE

__ __ __ (__) __ __ __ (__)

3. sung or played with short, clear-cut tones: CATSCOAT

__ __ __ __ __ __ __ (__)

4. increase in volume of sound: CORDSCENE

___ ___ (___) ___ (___) ___ ___ ___ ___

5. composition of dances: GRAYPORCHHOE

___ ___ ___ ___ ___ (___) ___ ___ ___ ___ ___ ___

6. the final outcome of a literary plot: MOUNTENEED

___ ___ (___) (___) ___ ___ ___ ___ ___ ___

7. place where art objects are exhibited: USEMUM

___ ___ ___ ___ ___ (___)

8. the pattern of movement in music: MRTHHY

___ ___ (___) ___ ___ ___

9. an art expert: NOONCRUISES

___ ___ ___ ___ ___ (___) ___ (___) ___ ___ ___

10. experimental form of art: TANVA-RAGED

___ ___ ___ ___ ___-___ (___) ___ ___ ___

11. comparison of two things using the words *like* or *as*: LIMESI

___ ___ ___ ___ (___) ___

12. fantasy or playfulness used in art or literature: MYWISH

(___) ___ ___ ___ ___ ___

13. well-read or learned people: TIETRIAL

___ ___ ___ ___ ___ (___) ___ ___

14. exaggeration used in literature: LERYPHOBE

___ (___) ___ ___ ___ ___ ___ ___ ___

15. brief summary of a play: CARNOISE

(___) ___ ___ ___ ___ ___ ___ ___

16. using elaborate and complex ornamentation: QUOBARE

(___) ___ ___ ___ ___ ___ (___)

17. revival of the arts in 17th-century Europe: CRANIASENSE

___ ___ ___ (___) ___ ___ ___ ___ ___ ___ ___

18. unnatural and fantastic imagery in art and literature: RARESUS-LIM

___ (___) ___ ___ ___ ___ ___ ___ ___ ___

19. artist who fashions three-dimensional works of art: CURLSTOP

___ ___ ___ ___ ___ (___) ___ ___

20. dramatic monologue: YOSOQUILL

___ ___ ___ ___ ___ ___ ___ ___ (___)

QUOTATION:

“___ ___ A ___ ___, ___ ___ ___ ___ ___ ___ ___
___ ___ A ___ ___ A ___ ___
___ ___ A ___ ___ ___.”

A PERSONAL LIST OF SPELLING DEMONS

In this section write all the words in this chapter with which you had problems. Study your list carefully before going on to the review section that follows. You can also use this page as a continuing spelling reference, adding new words as you come across them.

EXERCISES FOR REVIEW

A. There are eight spelling errors in the following passage. Cross out each misspelled word and write the correct spelling above it.

The United States government is a representitive democrasy based on constitutional rights. The federal government is composed of three branches. The executive and legislative branches are elected by majoraty vote. The judiciary is appointed by the president. Canidates for president are selected at political conventions by delagates of their own party. The American economic system is a capitalist one, but the government does not take a laissez-faire attitude toward the economy. Much of the federal buraucracy exists to regulate business and financial matters.

In a totalatarian society, the government controls every aspect of life. Some dictators espouse communist principles, while others practice fascizm. In a dictatorship the people cannot choose their leaders. Often change comes only through a military coup d'état.

B. The following magazine article contains ten spelling errors. Cross out each misspelled word and write the correct spelling above it.

Is the summer heat keeping you out of the kitchen? Do you miss those yummy casserolls and quiches of cooler days? Well, you don't need to turn on the oven to turn out a good home-cooked meal. This quick stove-top supper is chock full of the flavor and nutrition of good fresh vegtables.

Stir fry small bits of boneless chicken for five minutes or until cooked through. Then sauté chopped broccoli and zuccini in margerine. Add the cooked chicken and sprinkle on grated mozarella or parmesan cheese. Serve over spagetti.

Add a crispy salad with vinaigrette dressing, and you've got a deliciously satisfying summer meal. For desert serve fresh fruits (rasberries and cantalopes are beautiful this time of year) and iced cappucino with cinammon.

C. The following paragraph contains eight spelling errors. Cross out each misspelled word and write the correct spelling above it.

Connisseurs of the arts use knowledge and sensitivity to judge oeuvres from different forms. A person knowledgeable about painting is aware of historical movements such as impressionism and surealism and may keep up with the latest avant-guard techniques as well. A music expert is sensitive to the gradual change from crescendo to diminuendo in a piece and can describe the rhythym as staccato or legato. A drama critic uses specific criteria to judge the effectiveness of a protaganist's soliloquy in a tradegy. And a ballet enthusiast learns to appreciate how movements such as arabesks, entrechats, and pirouettes seem to flow effortlessly in good coreography.

D. The following paragraph contains five spelling errors. Cross out each misspelled word and write the correct spelling above it.

The defendent was arraigned today. He was indited on the felony charge of grand larseny. The prosecuter will subpoena five witnesses. She will warn them all of the penalties for perjery.

E. The following paragraph contains six spelling errors. Cross out each misspelled word and write the correct spelling above it.

My family doctor is a specialist in caring about people. She will patiently answer any questions I have about anatomy and physiology. She is as gentle as possible with the hypodermic needle when she gives innoculations and other injections. She will listen to my complaints about aches and pains without thinking I'm a hypocondriac. She is very careful about prescribing drugs such as antihistimines, barbiturates, and penacillin. And she is a firm believer in preventive medicine. She strongly recommends airobic exercise and a low cholesterall diet to keep one's cardiovascular system healthy and prevent hypertension.

F. The following paragraph contains five spelling errors. Cross out each misspelled word and write the correct spelling above it.

Most of us have to borrow money at some time in our lives. The biggest debt in many people's lives is the morgage on a house. This loan is usually amortized over twenty or thirty years. In the early years most of a house payment goes toward paying intrest on the loan rather than decreasing the principle. The person or institution that grants a loan is called the creditor. The creditor often asks for collateral before approving a loan. Creditors may even acquire a lean on the borrower's property. Persons who can no longer pay their debts may sell all their property and declare bankrupcy.

6. MASTERY TESTS

Here's your chance to test yourself and review what you have learned in your study of this book. The Mastery Tests begin with Chapter 2 and continue through Chapter 5. If you come across any stumbling blocks, go back to the chapter and review the topic in which you need additional work. Then try the Mastery Test again.

2. THE VARIETIES OF ENGLISH

A. Each sentence is an example of *formal, standard, informal,* or *substandard* language. In each blank, write the type of language used in that sentence. One answer will be used twice.

__________ **1.** I see where they're going ahead with the plan irregardless of what the governor says.

__________ **2.** Should a company be held responsible for injuries caused by its products?

__________ **3.** "Prudence, indeed, will dictate that governments long-established should not be changed for light and transient causes. . . ."

__________ **4.** There's no doubt but what you hadn't ought to do that.

__________ **5.** Give us a break and don't be such a stuffed shirt, okay?

B. Each of the following sentences contains either *jargon,* a *regionalism,* a *euphemism,* or *sexist language.* In each blank, write the type of language used in that sentence. One answer will be used twice.

__________ **1.** An acoustic coupler is a type of modem used in data transmissions to convert digital into acoustic signals and vice versa.

__________ 2. My grandmother passed away last year.

__________ 3. I love to eat flapjacks for breakfast.

__________ 4. It takes courage to be a fireman or a policeman.

__________ 5. Nine out of ten doctors recommend this product for occasional irregularity.

C. Each term below is often used as a euphemism for a blunter, more explicit term. "Translate" each euphemism by writing a more explicit term for it in the blank.

1. preowned __________
2. expectorate __________
3. "adult" (movie, bookstore) __________
4. discomfort __________
5. sanitation engineer __________
6. exceptional (child) __________
7. perspire __________
8. bathroom bowl __________
9. memorial park __________
10. senior citizen __________
11. under the influence __________
12. social disease __________
13. pass away __________

D. Match each of the following slang expressions with its counterpart in standard English.

____	1. hack it	a.	mentally prepared
____	2. freak (n.)	b.	a failure
____	3. flack	c.	exaggerated praise
____	4. hype	d.	ignore
____	5. fink	e.	succeed, cope
____	6. to get a kick out of	f.	tense

____ **7.** psyched **g.** enthusiast, fan

____ **8.** uptight **h.** enjoy, appreciate

____ **9.** to give the cold shoulder **i.** criticism

____ **10.** all washed up **j.** informer

E. Read the following excerpt from the dictionary entry for *take*. Then read sentences 1–12 below. If the sentence demonstrates a colloquial or slang usage of the word *take*, write *informal* in the blank. If the sentence does not contain a colloquial or slang usage, write *standard* in the blank.

—☆**on the take** [Slang] willing or seeking to take bribes or illicit income —**take after** **1.** to be, act, or look like **2.** to run after or pursue: also **take out** (or **off**) **after** —**take amiss** **1.** orig., to be wrong concerning; mistake **2.** to misunderstand the reason behind (an act), esp. so as to become offended —**take back** **1.** to regain use or possession of **2.** to retract (something said, promised, etc.) **3.** to return (something), as to be exchanged —**take down** **1.** to remove from a higher place and put in a lower one; pull down **2.** to unfasten; take apart **3.** to make less conceited; humble **4.** to put in writing; record —☆**take five** (or **ten,** etc.) take a five (or ten, etc.) minute break, as from working —**take for** **1.** to consider to be; regard as **2.** to mistake for —**take in** **1.** to admit; receive **2.** to shorten (a sail) by reefing or furling **3.** to make smaller or more compact **4.** to include; comprise **5.** to understand; comprehend **6.** to cheat; trick; deceive ☆**7.** to visit [to *take in* all the sights] **8.** to receive into one's home for pay [to *take in* boarders] —**take it** **1.** to suppose; believe ☆**2.** [Slang] to withstand difficulty, criticism, hardship, ridicule, etc. —**take it or leave it** accept it or not —**take it out of** [Colloq.] **1.** to exhaust; tire **2.** to obtain payment or satisfaction from —☆**take it out on** [Colloq.] to make (another) suffer for one's own anger, irritation, bad temper, etc. —**take off** **1.** to remove (a garment, etc.) **2.** to draw or conduct away **3.** *a*) to go away; depart *b*) to absent oneself, as from work **4.** to deduct; subtract **5.** to kill **6.** to make a copy or likeness of **7.** to leave the ground or water in flight: said of an airplane **8.** [Colloq.] to start **9.** [Colloq.] to imitate in a burlesque manner; mimic —**take on** **1.** to acquire; assume (form, quality, etc.) **2.** to employ; hire **3.** to begin to do (a task, etc.); undertake **4.** to play against; oppose **5.** [Colloq.] to show violent emotion, especially anger or sorrow —**take one's time** to be slow or unhurried; delay —**take out** **1.** to remove; extract **2.** to obtain by application to the proper authority **3.** [Colloq.] to escort **4.** *Bridge* to bid higher than (one's partner) but in a different suit —**take over** to begin controlling, managing, etc.

__________ **1.** When the going got rough, I just couldn't *take it,* so I quit the team.

__________ **2.** Jack *takes after* his father in many ways.

__________ **3.** Their comedy routine was a *take off* on a famous movie.

__________ **4.** When will Consolidated *take over* your company?

__________ **5.** I *take it* you are not planning to go.

__________ **6.** Why don't you *take out* Laura?

__________ **7.** Don't *take it out on* him!

__________ **8.** *Take off* your coat and hang it in the closet.

__________ **9.** Do you think that politician is *on the take*?

__________ **10.** You can't *take back* your angry words now.

__________ **11.** She was *taken for* a sales clerk in the store.

__________ **12.** We were *taken in* by an unscrupulous merchant.

F. Arrange each group of synonyms from the MOST FORMAL to the LEAST FORMAL by writing the proper letters in the columns to the right. The first item has been done for you.

		Most Formal	*Standard*	*Least Formal*
1.	**a.** skill **b.** proficiency **c.** know-how	b	a	c
2.	**a.** err **b.** mess up **c.** make a mistake			
3.	**a.** avoid **b.** eschew **c.** steer clear of			
4.	**a.** pizzazz **b.** spirit **c.** elan			
5.	**a.** odd **b.** eccentric **c.** flaky			
6.	**a.** flick **b.** movie **c.** film			
7.	**a.** depart **b.** beat it **c.** go away			
8.	**a.** fool **b.** deceive **c.** pull the wool over			
9.	**a.** overcome **b.** surmount **c.** lick			
10.	**a.** asleep **b.** dormant **c.** dead to the world			

G. Rewrite each sentence in the space provided by changing the sexist language to more acceptable terminology.

1. Man must learn to control his frightening capacity for violence.

   ____

2. Most airlines offer special services to businessmen who are frequent fliers.

   ____

3. The ladies joined the men for dinner.

   ____

4. The lady salesman opened her sample case.

   ____

5. We are currently suffering from a shortage of manpower at the office.

   ____

6. What qualifications does a person need to be a good congressman?

   ____

7. I'll have my girl call your office in the morning.

   ____

8. She is known as one of the finest craftsmen in the area.

   ____

9. A sweet young thing was sitting alone in the restaurant.

   ____

10. She is a noted poetess and authoress.

    ____

H. The language in two of the following passages maintains a consistent tone throughout. Find these passages and write CONSISTENT in the blanks next to them. The remaining passages contain a few words that disrupt their overall tone. For these passages, write INCONSISTENT in the blanks. Then circle the inappropriate words.

______________ **1.** We must adhere to the most stringent standards of excellence in our evaluations. Such standards will demonstrate to everyone concerned that our students are not just goofing off and coasting through courses that are pieces of cake.

______________ **2.** Amy can't hack those hyped up, glitzy resorts that rip off tourists. Give her a laid-back, mellow scene where she can just cool out.

______________ **3.** I get a kick out of pulling his leg, and he's the type of guy who doesn't freak out or anything when he finds out you're putting him on. His affability and equanimity are the attributes I admire most in him.

______________ **4.** Many volunteer organizations contribute to the success and pride of our community. Being as how these organizations are so important, it ain't right to criticize their efforts.

______________ **5.** Regardless of anyone's assertions to the contrary, Steve still maintains that lack of strategy was the primary cause of his defeat.

I. In each group there are three words that represent the same level or variety of English and one word that does not. Circle the word that does not belong in each group.

1. ain't, anywheres, isn't, irregardless
2. plastered, smashed, bombed, intoxicated
3. flapjack, chill bumps, teeter-totter, television

4. memorial park, spit, bathroom bowl, preowned

5. salesman, business executive, firefighter, repairer

6. wife, woman, young woman, weaker sex

7. pooped, bushed, exhausted, wiped out

8. loaded, wealthy, affluent, prosperous

9. disk drive, byte, information, printout

10. rang, fought, chose, brung

3. FINDING A SYNONYM

A. One synonym in each pair has an unfavorable connotation. Circle that synonym.

1. curious, prying

2. horde, host

3. facile, effortless

4. renowned, notorious

5. betray, disclose

B. Circle the best answer to each question.

1. Which synonym suggests stronger favorable connotations?
a. noted **b.** illustrious

2. Which synonym often implies a moral judgment?
a. repudiate **b.** decline

3. Which synonym better describes a talented person who is not conceited or boastful?
a. bashful **b.** modest

4. Which synonym implies a stronger degree of certainty?
a. possible **b.** likely

5. Which synonym implies anger?
a. glare **b.** gaze

C. Each word defined below is one of the synonyms you studied in Chapter 3. Read each definition and write the correct word in the blank. Choose your answers from the Word List below. If you need additional help, turn back to Chapter 3.

1. habitually curious and prone to persistent questioning

____

2. easily and quickly achieved, but perhaps lacking thoroughness and depth ________________

3. to disclose what should be kept secret or private ________________

4. a moving crowd of people pushing one another ________________

5. a large predatory group ________________

6. having a reputation based on brilliance of achievement

____

7. to disown, disavow, or condemn ________________

8. to reject with contempt or disdain ________________

9. shy in an embarrassed and awkward way ________________

10. to attempt something with earnest exertion ________________

Word List

horde	divulge
bashful	spurn
facile	illustrious
strive	repudiate
inquisitive	throng

D. Using the dictionary

1. Read the following dictionary excerpt. Then answer questions a–d.

> ***SYN.*—opponent,** an unemotional word, refers to anyone who is opposed to one, as in a fight, game, debate, etc.; **antagonist** implies more active opposition, especially in a struggle for control or power; **adversary** usually suggests actual hostility in the conflict; **enemy** may imply actual hatred in the opponent and a desire to injure, or it may simply refer to any member of the opposing group, nation, etc., whether or not there is personal animosity or hostility involved; **foe,** now a somewhat literary synonym for **enemy,** connotes more active hostility —***ANT.*** **ally, confederate**

a. Which synonym implies a struggle for power? ______________

b. Which synonym is the least emotional? ______________

c. Which three synonyms may imply hostility or hatred?

______________, ______________, ______________

d. Which of the synonyms listed in **c.** is somewhat formal or literary?

____

2. Read the following dictionary excerpt. Then answer questions a–e.

> ***SYN.***—**artificial** is applied to anything made by human work, esp. if in imitation of something natural *[artificial hair]*; **synthetic** is applied to a substance that is produced by chemical synthesis and is used as a substitute for a natural substance which it resembles *[synthetic dyes]*; **ersatz,** which refers to an artificial substitute, always implies an inferior substance *[ersatz coffee made of acorns]*; **counterfeit** and **spurious** are applied to a careful imitation deliberately intended to deceive *[counterfeit money, a spurious signature]* —***ANT.*** **natural**

a. Which word is often used to describe plastics and certain chemically produced fabrics? ______________

b. Which word would you use to describe imitation butter or cream that doesn't taste as good as the real thing? ______________

c. Which word is often used to describe money that is not authentic?

____

d. Which word is the most general? ______________

e. Which is the best word to describe a forgery? ______________

E. Look up each of the following words in a thesaurus. Write down as many synonyms as you can find for each one. Then use your dictionary—or your own knowledge of shades of meaning—to select the best synonym to complete each sentence.

1. throw: ______________

____

We will ______________ our fishing lines into the water.

2. inhabitant: ______________________________

____

A ______________ is someone who settles on unoccupied land without having right or title to it.

3. predicament: ______________________________

____

A person facing a ______________ must choose between two equally disagreeable alternatives.

4. discuss: ______________________________

____

The candidates will ______________ the issues on television on Monday night.

5. rebellion: ______________________________

____

The sailors plotted a ______________ to take over the ship.

F. In each blank write the synonym that best completes the sentence. Always choose a precise or vivid word rather than a bland, general one. When there is more than one precise synonym listed, choose the one that best fits the meaning of the sentence.

1. The thief ______________ my purse. (Choices: took, snatched, removed)
2. We ______________ down a peaceful country lane. (Choices: strolled, walked, scrambled)
3. He ______________ in wonder at the spectacular sight. (Choices: looked, glared, gazed)
4. She had a(n) ______________ experience on her trip. (Choices: bad, unpleasant, awful)
5. The novel had a ______________ ending. (Choices: dramatic, good, nice)

6. We came upon a deserted ______________ in the woods. (Choices: building, dwelling, cabin)

7. The old friends ______________ for hours at the reunion. (Choices: talked, reminisced, conversed)

8. It's fun to try to ______________ the future. (Choices: imagine, think about, recollect)

9. He raced to the table, ______________ his food, and was gone in a matter of minutes. (Choices: ate, savored, bolted)

10. In just one day, stock prices ______________ from an all-time high to an all-time low. (Choices: plummeted, fell, descended)

11. The trapeze artist nervously ______________ the bar. (Choices: took hold of, held onto, gripped)

12. An architect's model is a ______________ version of a building. (Choices: small, miniature, petite)

G. Two of the words in each group are synonyms. One is not. Circle the word that does not belong in each group. All of the words are ones you studied in Chapter 3.

1. meddlesome, prying, diffident
2. facile, easy, notorious
3. repudiate, reveal, disclose
4. spurn, divulge, betray
5. throng, attempt, swarm
6. inquisitive, renowned, eminent
7. probable, likely, simple
8. endeavor, reject, essay
9. modest, demure, famous
10. betray, stare, peer

4. HOMONYMS AND OTHER CONFUSING WORDS

A. In each sentence, underline the correct word of each pair in parentheses.

1. Janice works in the (personal/personnel) department as the medical benefits manager.
2. The team's (moral/morale) was high after winning the last game of the season.
3. We had good seats in the (forth/fourth) row.
4. Don't (flaunt/flout) your gold jewelry on the train.
5. It's (poring/pouring) outside.
6. I bought some notebooks at the (stationary/stationery) store.
7. Her doctor (prescribed/proscribed) a new medication.
8. The computer has (dual/duel) disk drives.
9. Who caught the (bridal/bridle) bouquet?
10. She put on the (brakes/breaks) and came to a complete stop.
11. It's foolish to (morn/mourn) for the good old days.
12. He climbed into the upper (berth/birth) and went to sleep.
13. Some of the (gorilla/guerrilla) fighters in the revolution are young boys.
14. We drove (threw/through) the tunnel.
15. Do you know (whether/weather) he's arriving tonight?
16. I don't know (wear/where) to park.
17. Can you give him some good (advice/advise)?
18. The company is making (incredible/incredulous) claims for that product.
19. Overly (credible/credulous) consumers may often be cheated.
20. The radio station gave away (complementary/complimentary) tickets to the concert.
21. It is your (right/rite) to see your attorney.
22. His (principal/principle) concern is for your safety.

23. We saw a red (flair/flare) burning along the side of the highway.

24. Only a very clever person could dream up such an (ingenious/ingenuous) plan.

25. Have you (shone/shown) everyone your award?

26. He was the (sole/soul) survivor of the plane crash.

27. A (pain/pane) of glass was shattered by the high winds.

28. Every citizen has a right to be free from (persecution/prosecution).

29. The kite (soared/sored) over the trees.

30. Was Raoul (born/borne) in the United States?

B. Twenty homonyms from Chapter 4 are defined below. A rhyming clue has been given for each word. Spell each homonym correctly in the blank. The first one has been done for you.

1. unit of instruction (Clue: rhymes with *horse*) course

2. Marine ______ or ______ de ballet (Clue: rhymes with *bore*) ______

3. a sheet of glass (Clue: rhymes with *reign*) ______

4. uninterested (Clue: rhymes with *lord*) ______

5. in this place (Clue: rhymes with *beer*) ______

6. not fancy (Clue: rhymes with *vein*) ______

7. if (Clue: rhymes with *leather*) ______

8. at what place (Clue: rhymes with *share*) ______

9. in one side and out the other (Clue: rhymes with *chew*) ______

10. ______ geometry (Clue: rhymes with *brain*) ______

11. part of the body (Clue: rhymes with *chased*) ______

12. seven days (Clue: rhymes with *shriek*) ______

13. combat between two persons (Clue: rhymes with *cruel*) ______

14. governing body, council (Clue: rhymes with *cord*) ______

15. to withstand, endure (Clue: rhymes with *hair*) ______

C. Crossword Confusion: Use the definitions below to fill in the spaces of this crossword puzzle. Most of the answers are taken from the lists of homonyms and other confusing words in Chapter 4. Refer to those lists if you need help.

ACROSS

1. route
4. unclothed
6. king's chair
8. unit of weight for gems
11. source of metals
12. light in color
13. The Wizard ___ Oz
15. past tense of *lead*
16. permitted
18. sick
19. antonym for *live*
23. 6th note of the scale
25. what a belt goes around
27. change
31. was aware of
34. abbreviation for *road*
35. not tight
36. tooth covering
38. antonym for *war*
40. evaluate
41. give advice
42. more unusual
44. most despicable
45. 1/100 of a dollar
46. row
47. smell, odor
49. to perceive sounds
51. part of a play
52. rob
53. caustic chemical
54. endure, withstand
55. victim of a predator
56. go around or turn over and over
57. antonym for *old*

DOWN

1. breakfast food
2. transmitted
3. made smooth & level
4. uninterested
5. 2nd note of the scale
7. part played by an actor
8. money for investment
9. not artificial
10. past tense of *tell*
14. thin sheet of aluminum
17. not strong
20. editor's mark
21. peg pounded into the ground
22. in that order
24. female chicken
26. not busy
28. ___ and behold!
29. opposite of *from*
30. type of fishing gear
32. requires
33. goods for sale
37. market
39. rough
41. mention
43. abandon
44. exist
45. to make complete
48. all of the actors in a play
50. transportation fee
55. opening in the skin

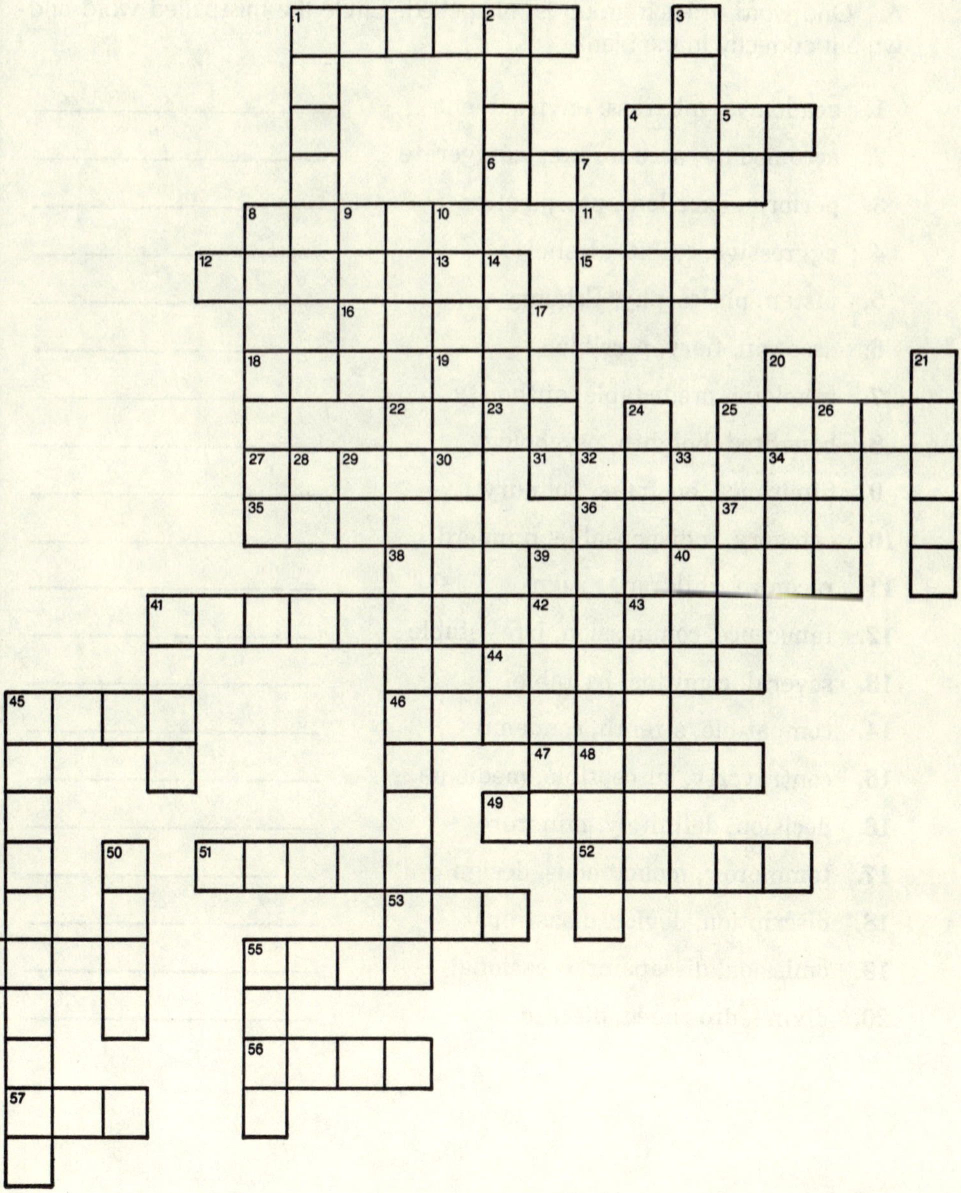

5. TROUBLE-SHOOTING FOR GOOD SPELLING

A. One word in each group is misspelled. Circle the misspelled word and write it correctly in the blank.

1. academy, embarass, environment ____________
2. accomodate, accumulate, exaggerate ____________
3. perform, excellent, prespiration ____________
4. aggressive, exibit, alcohol ____________
5. fasten, philosophy, Febuary ____________
6. assassin, fiery, possible ____________
7. atheletic, predictable, authority ____________
8. benefited, heighth, psychology ____________
9. hindrance, business, boundry ____________
10. category, indispensable, hunderd ____________
11. reconize, children, resign ____________
12. innocence, commission, irresistable ____________
13. several, comittee, irritable ____________
14. compatible, strenth, condemn ____________
15. contraversy, susceptible, medicine ____________
16. decision, definitely, minature ____________
17. tommorow, monotonous, design ____________
18. discription, device, disastrous ____________
19. omission, dissapoint, occasional ____________
20. divine, drownded, disease ____________

B. WORD SEARCH: Government and Politics

The words in the list below are hidden in this puzzle. Circle each word you find. Words can read in any direction.

D	E	L	E	F	A	S	C	I	S	M	J	U	D	M	L	S	E	R
E	C	O	N	S	E	E	R	S	T	C	H	I	A	C	A	D	L	E
M	C	I	E	A	V	T	F	W	Q	J	H	J	R	Y	I	Z	E	N
R	O	D	A	S	S	A	B	M	A	D	Q	I	C	B	S	I	W	R
A	N	E	C	I	R	G	Y	P	A	V	O	B	E	X	Y	A	G	E
T	S	O	O	H	X	E	U	R	N	J	G	I	P	C	H	F	R	P
Y	T	L	N	T	C	L	J	O	A	O	O	B	A	K	L	I	O	R
C	I	O	S	V	N	E	S	L	H	I	Z	R	W	R	A	B	Y	E
A	T	G	E	T	A	D	I	D	N	A	C	X	I	F	N	N	C	S
R	U	Y	N	U	D	M	E	T	S	U	D	I	Z	T	O	A	Z	E
C	T	J	S	K	L	U	I	M	A	F	N	E	D	D	Y	C	O	N
O	I	C	U	R	M	T	V	E	O	Y	S	E	K	U	O	X	S	T
M	O	O	S	T	A	I	R	M	R	S	K	R	P	S	J	J	W	A
E	N	N	T	Y	U	U	B	R	I	E	C	R	U	O	C	A	L	T
D	A	E	I	O	B	R	T	A	T	E	D	P	U	O	C	I	R	I
B	L	A	T	O	T	A	L	I	T	A	R	I	A	N	A	G	R	V
P	D	F	D	Q	U	T	G	E	L	E	I	D	U	J	M	F	C	E

Word List

ambassador	delegates	laissez-faire
bureaucracy	democracy	majority
candidate	fascism	representative
consensus	ideology	totalitarian
constitutional	judiciary	

C. WORD SEARCH: Food and Cooking

The words in the list below are hidden in this puzzle. Circle each word you find. Words can read in any direction.

C	I	N	I	H	C	C	U	Z	C	R	O	S	N	M
I	Q	U	L	C	A	P	P	U	C	C	I	N	O	A
N	R	Y	O	G	U	R	T	R	A	Z	L	I	H	C
N	A	S	C	I	N	N	O	L	L	I	U	O	B	M
A	B	P	C	H	O	C	O	L	A	T	E	C	H	O
M	M	A	O	C	A	N	T	D	E	S	E	R	N	Z
O	A	G	R	T	U	F	R	L	Q	U	A	F	I	Z
N	Y	H	B	A	R	B	E	C	U	E	M	G	T	A
A	O	E	I	R	P	M	S	G	I	Q	A	C	N	R
E	N	T	S	L	O	P	S	B	C	S	R	O	A	E
I	N	T	B	P	A	L	E	C	H	O	A	F	S	L
M	A	I	E	N	O	S	D	T	E	N	G	F	S	L
C	I	N	T	B	R	O	C	H	I	L	I	E	I	A
J	S	N	R	V	E	G	A	V	C	Z	N	E	O	D
D	E	C	A	F	F	E	I	N	A	T	E	D	R	K
E	B	G	O	Y	R	R	E	B	P	S	A	R	C	H

Word List

appetizer
barbecue
bouillon
broccoli
cappuccino
chili
chocolate
cinnamon
coffee
croissant
decaffeinated
dessert
lasagne
mayonnaise
mozzarrella
quiche
raspberry
spaghetti
yogurt
zucchini

D. WORD SEARCH: Health and Medicine

The words in the list below are hidden in this puzzle. Circle each word you find. Words can read in any direction.

```
C H A N A T O M Y R A E H R R A I D C
H Y P O D E R M I C A R T A N O C C R
O T S I G E L O M A H D H P O A R A O
C A R T I L A G E I Y H E M R A M N M
H N D A R H I C A N G N O C T E P O T
I T I L C L Y A I N I R I N Z O E D S
R I A U R H Y P O B N N S C C P D N I
O H N C H R O M O S O M E T O T I O G
P I A O O T A L I G B R X S N H A C O
R S T N I L T C E R P E E T G E T R L
A T A I N E E N B S S Y N A E M R E O
C A B A R B I N O N T E L I N I I P C
T M I E G A H R R O M E H S I G C Y E
O I P A R A L Y S I S O R T T E I H N
R N A I C I R T E T S B O O A X A N Y
R E P M E H Y P E N I C I L L I N O G
```

Word List

aerobic	chromosome	inoculation
anatomy	congenital	obstetrician
antihistamine	diarrhea	paralysis
carcinogen	eczema	pediatrician
cartilage	gynecologist	penicillin
chiropractor	hemorrhage	
cholesterol	hypodermic	

E. One word in each group is misspelled. Circle the misspelled word and write it correctly in the blank.

1. parallel, parlament, possession ____________________
2. adress, phenomenon, bookkeeper ____________________
3. probly, responsibility, stalk ____________________
4. surprise, temperature, apolagize ____________________
5. government, inevitable, quantity ____________________
6. mathematics, devide, despair ____________________
7. necessary, occurence, different ____________________

8. broccoli, casserole, concensus ______________________
9. candidate, bankrupcy, collateral ______________________
10. raspberry, zucchini, morgage ______________________
11. choclate, connoisseur, affidavit ______________________
12. hemorrhage, mayonnaise, defendent ______________________
13. staccato, protaganist, temperament ______________________
14. aerobic, diarrhea, colesterol ______________________
15. bureaucracy, ambassader, subpoena ______________________

F. WORD SEARCH: Business and Finance

The words in the list below are hidden in this puzzle. Circle each word you find. Words can read in any direction.

A	T	U	Y	C	T	P	U	R	K	N	A	B	I	T	O	R
M	P	R	G	A	O	I	P	A	C	C	R	U	E	P	E	R
E	I	S	O	N	E	L	A	R	M	B	A	N	A	R	N	O
R	E	E	P	T	C	O	L	A	O	O	R	I	N	E	T	T
T	C	E	I	N	P	L	E	A	R	E	R	A	N	S	R	E
N	E	G	O	T	S	E	R	E	T	N	I	T	U	E	E	I
E	R	D	E	P	R	G	A	G	G	E	P	R	I	R	P	R
G	A	P	R	I	N	C	I	P	A	L	R	O	T	Z	R	P
O	L	L	O	R	A	C	R	E	G	I	D	A	Y	L	E	O
T	E	N	T	P	E	R	R	S	E	E	E	I	L	I	N	R
I	T	O	I	N	E	G	O	L	E	N	N	O	S	R	E	P
A	I	T	D	E	P	R	E	C	I	A	T	I	O	N	U	I
B	A	R	E	T	O	N	Y	R	O	S	S	I	M	O	R	P
L	L	A	R	R	E	A	R	S	C	H	A	N	A	R	N	A
E	P	L	C	M	E	R	C	H	A	N	D	I	S	E	O	N

Word List

accrue
amortize
annuity
arrears
bankruptcy
capital
collateral
creditor
depreciation
entrepreneur
interest
lien
merchandise
mortgage
negotiable
personnel
principal
promissory note
proprietor
receipt

G. WORD SEARCH: Law

The words in the list below are hidden in this puzzle. Circle each word you find. Words can read in any direction.

A	N	E	G	L	I	G	E	N	C	E	J	M	I	S	E	T
S	U	P	E	N	A	R	R	A	N	J	U	R	Y	F	O	R
A	L	A	R	O	T	U	C	E	S	O	R	P	E	N	A	O
Y	F	E	L	L	A	N	I	T	H	E	I	D	E	F	H	N
N	G	I	A	R	R	A	H	N	T	N	S	E	F	O	I	A
E	Y	N	O	L	E	F	O	A	D	X	D	A	M	A	N	E
C	A	D	E	F	E	F	C	D	L	I	I	I	Y	S	D	M
R	M	N	Y	Z	L	I	E	N	V	L	C	P	B	O	I	E
A	D	A	R	B	D	D	N	E	P	I	T	T	S	R	T	D
L	P	B	U	U	M	A	C	F	D	N	I	S	M	P	O	S
P	E	T	J	L	I	V	G	E	O	E	O	A	F	E	R	I
R	L	D	R	T	S	I	R	D	Z	A	N	E	J	O	N	M
O	A	T	E	M	D	T	X	C	O	P	Y	R	I	G	H	T
S	U	B	P	O	E	N	A	B	L	E	M	E	N	P	E	R

Word List

adjudicate	felony	misdemeanor
affidavit	homicide	negligence
arraign	indictment	perjury
copyright	jurisdiction	prosecutor
defendant	larceny	subpoena

H. WORD SEARCH: The Arts

The words in the list below are hidden in this puzzle. Circle each word you find. Words can read in any direction.

A	M	C	R	E	S	C	E	N	D	O	B	C
S	E	L	O	D	E	F	A	E	R	N	E	G
O	T	I	G	N	R	H	M	I	A	R	L	B
L	A	M	J	E	N	K	E	L	M	H	I	A
I	P	A	S	N	O	O	N	P	A	Y	M	R
L	H	C	L	A	S	S	I	C	T	T	I	O
O	O	T	Q	U	R	T	C	S	I	H	S	Q
Q	R	I	O	M	E	M	W	V	S	M	S	U
U	A	C	Y	D	E	G	A	R	T	E	T	E
Y	H	P	A	R	G	O	I	B	O	T	U	A
D	R	E	C	N	A	S	S	I	A	N	E	R

Word List

autobiography
baroque
cinema
classic
climactic
connoisseur
crescendo
dramatist
fresco
genre
memoir
metaphor
renaissance
rhythm
simile
soliloquy
tragedy

INDEX

Page numbers in *italics* contain exercises related to main discussion.